Ezekiel

Back Then

Simple Pleasures and Everyday Heroes

Texas Heritage Series
Number Seven

Also in this series:

Christmas at the Ranch by Elmer Kelton

What I Learned on the Ranch by James Bruce Frazier

The Parramore Sketches by Dock Dilworth Parramore

A Small Town in Texas by Glenn Dromgoole

Biscuits O'Bryan by Monte Jones

Buffalo Days as told to James Winford Hunt

To Judy

who shares the memories

Back Then

Simple Pleasures and Everyday Heroes

Archie P. McDonald

Cover painting by Kay Shannon

State House
Press

McMurry University
Abilene, Texas

Library of Congress Cataloging-in-Publication Data

McDonald, Archie P.
    Back then : simple pleasures and everyday heroes /
Archie P. Mcdonald
            p. cm.—(Texas heritage series ; no. 7)
        ISBN-13: 978-1-880510-81-0 (cloth : alk. paper)
        ISBN-10: 1-880510-81-2 (cloth : alk. paper)
1. Texas—Social life and customs—20th century—Anecdotes. 2.
McDonald, Archie P.—Anecdotes. 3. McDonald, Archie P.—Childhood
and youth—Anecdotes. 4. Texas—Biography—Anecdotes. 5.
UnitedStates—Social life and customs—
20th century—Anecdotes.
I. Title. II. Series.
    F386.6.M39 2005
    976.4'063—dc22

                                                    2005011248

State House Press
McMurry Station, Box 637
Abilene, TX 79697-0637
(325) 793-4682
www.mcwhiney.org

Distributed by Texas A&M University Press Consortium
www.tamu.edu/upress
1-800-826-8911

ISBN: 1-880510-81-2
10 9 8 7 6 5 4 3 2 1

Book Designed by Rosenbohm Graphic Design

Contents

Part II: Everyday Heroes

Photograph on page 17 is from the Buffalo Gap Historic Village.
All other photographs are from the author.

Introduction

These stories recall a time when a kid could go to the picture show with fifteen cents in his pocket, purchase admission for nine cents, and have money left over for popcorn. I do not argue that that time was "better." It was simply my time. Some of these thoughts may tickle your memory, too, or tell others about our corner of the world when we were young.

For more than five years, I have been broadcasting weekly commentaries like these for the Red River Radio network under the heading of "the Southern condition." RRR, a part of National Public Radio, headquarters on the campus of Louisiana State University, Shreveport, but has affiliates in central Louisiana, eastern Texas, and southern Arkansas, so I suppose we are as much Southwestern as Southern.

Every Friday morning we interrupt NPR's "Morning Edition" at 7:35 to broadcast my commentaries. The five-minute format allows me about three minutes and leaves program manager Adam Giblin a minute or so on each end to announce what is about to happen and to remind listeners that it did.

My middle minutes are most often autobiographical. This is not the result of narcissus; rather, it is the reservoir upon which I draw for memories of summer evenings, vacation Bible schools, favorite relatives, or whatever seems right for a particular Friday.

Subjects vary, but reviewing them now, what seems to emerge is a kind of report of what it was like to live in Texas, or the South, a half century ago.

Archie P. McDonald

Part I:
Simple Pleasures

Simpler Times

Recently I read a book titled *The Sixties*, which provided a review of a tumultuous decade that featured civil rights, gender and sexual revolutions, and significant protests against our nation's involvement in Vietnam. The introductory chapter dealt with the '50s, and its purpose was to emphasize that decades' alleged buttoned-down, Levittown sameness and calm—a kind of quiet before the stormy '60s. As author Terry Anderson said, "...life was good, and it was simple, during Happy Days."

Baloney. This is a good example of how generalities distort specifics. Terry must not have been fifteen years old in 1950 and worried about everything concerning his own physical and social development when that decade started. Let's imagine a kid, pimpled, string-bean thin at six feet and weighing about 140 pounds, a big gap between his frontal incisors, uncontrollably wavy hair in an era of ducktails and pompadours, nerdy (though then he would have been called book wormy), with insufficient nerve to ask a girl to dance and anyway handicapped by two left feet. Life was, and is, never "good" or "simple" for such poor creatures.

You may have figured out that the portrait I have just described is autobiographical. Looking back, I judge that it all worked pretty

My freshman year at French High School.

well. That "book-wormy" nature led to college, then advanced degrees, and a professional career now stretching beyond four decades and early expectations. I finally met a girl with whom I could talk easily, who overlooked my lack of looks, and that "girl" and I just marked our forty-eighth wedding anniversary.

Looking at it from the front, I could have imagined none of this. From the perspective of the '50s—my teen time—I expected the world to blow itself to hell through nuclear fission, its people to battle each other in the streets over war and race without possible resolution short of genocide, and never to make more than $10,000 a year, if that much.

There are several points here. One is that every teenager has a pretty rough time of it, even if the times appear "calm" and "simple" for those who have survived years between childhood and maturity.

A second is that there really aren't any "calm" and "simple" decades; all of them feature unique challenges and opportunities.

And a third is that I am glad that my "between time" led me to now. Whatever problems there may be, I *don't* have to worry about getting my homework ready for Miss Cunningham and I *do* have a date for Saturday night.

Shoe Shines

I have some ideas about how a man should dress with which few agree in this age of casual attire. A professional man should wear a necktie with his shirt, superfluous as one may be. Socks are mandatory everywhere but the beach. A suit is preferable, but sports jacket and slacks will do. And a man *must* wear shined shoes.

Getting one's shoes shined these days is a chore. There are few places where a man can go for this service anymore, so he is condemned to get out the Kiwi, an applicator rag or dauber, and a brush. Even then it looks "do-it-yourself" instead of professional.

Time was, every barbershop in America had a shoe-shine stand, and cities of any size hosted shine parlors. Barbershops usually had a single shoe-shine chair, but parlors featured a dozen or more. Either way, getting one's shoes shined professionally was an experience. For a boy metamorphosing into manhood, it was a passage.

When it was your turn—you often had to wait for this service—you took your scuffed self up onto a high seat. This was because a real professional shined the shoes while they were on your feet, so you had to elevate them to a reasonably comfortable working level for him. Once seated, you placed your feet on two little, miniature versions of shoe soles, bottom side up, about a foot apart. You hiked your pant legs a little to get them out of the way. Then you looked about as nonchalantly as you could manage while the pro applied saddle soap to clean the shoe, wiped it clean, slathered on a fresh coat of wax, and brushed it away to a shine—still dullish, but uniform and full of promise.

Then came the popping rag. These professionals could move that rag so fast across your shoes that you could feel the heat in your toes, and every now and then the pro arched the rag above your shoe and made it "pop" as it descended to add sparkle to leather. Last, he used somebody's old toothbrush to apply "sole dressing" around the edges of the lower part of the shoe.

All this time you stared at a symphony of skill on display at your feet and, for a while at least, you watched your step carefully to avoid marring a work of art.

Now I ask you: where can you get that much elegance for a quarter these days?

Shoe-shine chair

My fathers—plural—introduced me to this ritual. My natural father, who lived until I was eight years old, barbered some and I received free shines from my buddies in his shop. Later, my step-father often took me along on Sunday mornings to a shine parlor known as "Dummy's" because the operator was mute. I suppose that name would not be tolerated today. What I remember was that the proprietor for whom it was named provided a first-class shine.

In recent years I have seen shine stands in airports, but it isn't the same. Often the operators are girls. I believe in gender equality, but somehow that just doesn't seem right.

Hats

Time was, nearly everyone wore a hat. It was more than apparel. It was a tool. One of the classic Western paintings—a Russell or a Remington—features a cowpony drinking water from his rider's Stetson. A hat shades you from the sun's carcinogenic impact; or, if you live somewhere other than Texas, from the rain. As one who wears glasses, this is a valuable two-fer.

There are all kinds of utilitarian hats. Think of the hard hats worn by construction workers. In the 1970s, "hard hats" identified a group of Americans who were intolerant of hippies, war protestors, and other "untouchables." Cowboy hats, modified sombreros really, evidently must be white straw in summer and black felt in winter and worn at all times, even at the table. Uniform hats, especially for military members and servicepersons, are standards. Coach Tom Landry's hat became so familiar that when a stretch of highway was named for him, the highway sign sported an icon of his hat.

Wearing a hat while traveling with Judy.

The wearing of hats waned about 1960 when President John F. Kennedy chose to bear his tousled mane even in winter's cold. Now even the bald, who should know better, foreswear hats as well. Most of the non-hat wearers I know didn't or wouldn't have voted for Kennedy and will worry a little, now, to know they are emulating a Democrat.

I like hats. I must have about thirty of them and wear one daily. And I mean HATs, not caps. The fad in "gimme-caps"— the kind with the plastic adjuster in the back to make one size misfit all—is an advertiser's dream. Wearers are walking billboards. I don't understand that and am nearly offended by it. Especially if they are worn rally-style, bill backwards, as so many young folks do. Only baseball catchers and welders need to do that, or should.

What I like are *hats*—with a crown and a brim that goes all the way around. One should never leave home without one. Hats distinguish. They "dress up" the wearer. Protocol and courtesy while wearing them are required. Hats should be worn *outside,* not indoors, and *especially* never at the table. Wear straw when it is hot, felt or wool when it is not. It is all right to wear a hat into a building en route to an interior destination, but never in elevators. Gentlemen must remove their hats when Old Glory passes in parade, during public prayer in stadia or elsewhere, and—unless both hands are holding packages—when they greet ladies. All of this is old-fashioned, I know, but those are the rules, and I did say "gentlemen."

There is a problem with hats these days. If one follows the rule and removes one's bonnet upon entering a restaurant or a church, few of them provide a place to hang it. Once I sat beside a fellow hat wearer while attending a funeral service in a large urban church. These saints had spent many thousands of their tithes on the finest of organs, lush carpet, polished pews, and state-of-the-art sound system. But we two had to hold our hats in our laps while paying our respects to the departed. There was not so much as a nail in the wall to rest a hat while we did so. "Civilization lost something," my companion observed, "when hats went out of style."

The Corner Drug Store

A few years ago, Dr. Arthur Speck and I, on the occasion of cooling ourselves on an August evening in his swimming pool, amused ourselves by reviewing the transformation of the world during our lifetime, which spans about two-thirds of the last century.

Our parents began with real horsepower for transportation, yet lived to see, on television, Neil Armstrong walk on the moon. Our first telephones required the assistance of an operator to complete calls. We learned to dial our numbers on a rotary wheel. Then Touch-Tone sped the process, and a while ago I rode in a car accessorized with a voice activated and operated communications system. All this, folks, is progress.

I am not so sure I can agree that what has happened to drug stores is progress. Remember those emporiums, if you are old enough, the way Norman Rockwell painted them. And if you don't remember Norman Rockwell, I'll paint the picture for you.

They were not all on the corner, but we remember them best that way. There was a soda fountain, a gathering place where morning coffee was shared by area merchants, retirees, or others without much to do. At lunch, another crowd gathered for ham sandwiches and chips or maybe chili and crackers, accompanied by a Coke drawn from a fountain that mixed the syrup and carbonated water into a glass so familiar you could identify it blindfolded. They always tasted better than the bottled kind.

All kinds of wares lined shelves located along the walls or in short aisle-islands: patent medicine, jewelry, beauty aids, toys for the youngsters, walking canes for the old folks, paint, guitar strings—you were likely to find almost anything. Newspapers and magazines, which one could review without buying, occupied a rack. And in the back, usually elevated a bit, was the pharmacist who filled your prescriptions and gave advice on their use. Hundreds of bottles of liquids and pills of various colors or configurations—capsules, tablets, and powders—with mysterious healing properties, all in an order he seemed to understand thoroughly, surrounded him.

The pharmacist was a familiar, reassuring figure. You trusted him as completely as the doctor whose prescription you delivered because you grew up seeing him there, behind his counter. He lagniapped a peppermint for you when you visited with your parents, sent you home with his nostrums for ailing family, kept an eye out for your safety if a rough crowd dropped by after school. Later you appreciated his service on the school board, the town council, or some similar civic service.

And when you were grown, and *married*, and it was entirely proper unless you were Roman Catholic, you approached this trusted old friend, with some trepidation, and whispered, "Some prophylactics, please." Without a word or look of judgment, he fetched the product and presented it to you in a plain, non-plastic, non-transparent sack so the whole world didn't know your business.

I'll not forget the first time, in the 1980s, after the sexual revolution, when I first saw condoms hanging out there for selection between the foot powder and the Band-Aids. That meant, I suppose, that one in the market for such had to haul it to the checker—probably a teenaged girl—so the bar code could be scanned. God help you if she had to call on the loudspeaker for a price check.

Norman Rockwell and I do *not* regard this as "progress."

The Corner Grocery

It's big news in a small town when Wal-Mart announces plans to enlarge its discount center into a Superstore, or one of the supermarket chains opens or expands. These marketing giants dwarf the corner stands and stores of my earliest youth.

Growing up in the 1940s on Liberty Street in Beaumont, Texas, between Fourth and Fifth streets, offered two attractions in this line: one block south on Fourth was Hildreth's Grocery and a block away on Fifth stood Farasee's Grocery.

Hildreth's was more a "stand" than a store. Patrons did not enter. We approached an open-air sales counter and communicated our intended purchases to Mr. or Mrs. Hildreth, who fetched them to the counter. We buyers of Cokes and cones of ice cream preferred the services of Mrs. Hildreth, a diminutive lady with a pleasant face, to Old Man Hildreth, who had forsaken smiling for Lent in some long forgotten year and never got over it. We were, however, in awe of the loaded pistol he kept beside the cash register.

Joe Farasee kept a somewhat larger emporium, maybe twenty by thirty feet. There you could select your own canned beans, but the best features were the meat counter—you could watch Joe slice the meat and wrap it in butcher paper—and a large metal cabinet on the counter that had perhaps twelve panels with compartments on both sides. Each compartment featured a spring behind which Joe would place sales slips indicating a credit purchase. You settled with Joe on payday. Naturally, this was limited to adults unless Joe knew you were on an errand to fetch bread or milk for a busy mother.

Later on, after Old Man Hildreth and his pistol left, a man named Fertitta remodeled the stand into a modest store. He added an ice house, and there, in 1948, I entered the working world selling ice in twenty-five and fifty pound chunks to folks like my own who had yet to acquire an electric refrigerator and needed the frozen water to cool food stored in a genuine "ice box." I also peddled watermelons chilled in the icehouse, and learned to "plug" them to assure purchasers of ripeness. For this I was paid $1, in cash, at the end of each day. This, I am sure, was returned the following day, one soda pop or fudgecicle at a time.

The other day I bought an air-conditioner filter in a supermarket. I expect Old Man Hildreth would have reached for his pistol if I had tried to buy one from him back then.

Full Service Gas Stations

When I was a boy, we had only full-service gas stations. They were called "filling" stations because motorists primarily stopped there to refill automobile fuel tanks. You got that and more. Unless you needed to visit the toilet, which was usually clean and well stocked with soap and various tissues, or just stretch the legs, you could remain in the car.

The attendant, sometimes more than one, greeted you. "Fill'er up" was the command to commence the refueling. Or you might say, on account of economy, "Ten gallons," or even more specifically, "Five dollars' worth." You received that amount of gasoline—but also the rest of the service.

In my earliest days, the attendant "to and froed" the handle of a hand pump mounted near the base of a circular tower to elevate gasoline from a reservoir below the surface to a glass container atop the tower. The requested amount was gauged by gallon levels painted on the container. Then, with the hose nozzle secure in the neck leading to the car's fuel tank, he compressed the lever of the nozzle and allowed gravity to carry the product to its destination. All this became mechanized with electronic pumps, but for a while the rest of the "service" in service stations still functioned.

This involved "popping" the hood so the attendant could check the level of water in the radiator and add more if needed. In the days before complicated chemical radiator coolants, we used water. Only in winter was it laced with just enough anti-freeze to avoid a frozen block. Since many radiators leaked or boiled over, such periodic checks were beneficial.

Next he examined the dipstick to see if the motor had sufficient oil to keep it lubricated or if a quart needed to be added. He hoped it did, of course, since hardly anyone would refuse to purchase oil if told he "was about a quart low."

The attendant also checked the air pressure in the tires and, if you had stepped out of the car, whisked accumulated dirt and pebbles from the floor of the car with a little broom. Only then did the motorist relinquish the cash to pay for the gasoline. The service was free. And in some stations the serviceman even wore a little clip-on, leather, bow tie. All very elegant.

What genius decided that we should self-service ourselves? When this fad—now the norm—debuted, I'll admit I liked the speed and economy of pumping my own gas. But where is that guy who is supposed to tell me that I am "a quart low?"

Honky-Tonks

Words are interesting, and here is a good example: honky-tonks. This is not to be confused with "honkie," a pejorative reference to white persons (though I don't really know why). The "honky" in "tonks" has no "e" but I suspect it refers to a place where a lot of "l" can be raised.

I should say up front that any information I have about such places was gathered strictly in the spirit of historical and intellectual inquiry. A scholar must, after all, seek truth as close to the source as possible. In that spirit, then, I shall narrate a few visits to the seamy side, mostly made during my salad days, and one missed opportunity.

My first bona fide "honky-tonk" visits were tame. Here is an example. Along about sophomore time, I worked as a "gofer" on a National Linen Service truck that served the pleasure emporiums of Galveston. My duties involved exchanging fresh towel rolls in machines in restrooms. This was done in the early morning hours but not before all late-night patrons had departed or early risers arrived for an illegal pick-me-up to start the day. The roller machines were in women's as well as men's rooms, and the protocol was to knock, especially at the women's room, before entering. One fateful day a gravelly female voice called out, "Come on in, Honey." I've visited a few honky-tonks since, but with some apprehension.

Senior year. I joined several colleagues late of an evening in a run across the Sabine to a place called The Big Oak— again, just for research. One ordered some sweet, syrupy concoction, blood red. I remember the color going down, and it had hardly changed a bit when it came up on the inside of Danny Insurello's father's car because my friend couldn't get the window rolled down in time.

Over the years "research" has taken me to karaoke clubs in Japan, pubs in England and Australia, and bistros and brasseries on the Continent. Baptists don't go to such places at home, of course. After all this, I have reached some conclusions: people are pretty much the same all over the world. The dim light and loud music—especially country music— are props for the "good time" they seek to drive away the demons. Rarely, I suspect, does this actually work. But perhaps I haven't done enough research, which brings me to that lost opportunity.

A few years ago someone opened a joint called Playgirls at our county line. I'll let its title tickle your imagination about what was reported to occur within it. A publisher who let some of my columns appear in his newspaper invited several of us to accompany him there as investigative reporters, but we never did. He said it was our obligation as journalists. We were just too old, I suppose.

Sounds

Of all the senses, I suppose sight is the most precious. The loss of any of the senses—seeing, hearing, smelling, tasting, or feeling—is a burden, but it seems to me that sight is the most necessary for a fully actualized life.

But this is not to slight hearing. Sound makes possible a fun and profitable existence and, for me, stimulates memories. Visits to restored excursion trains such as the Texas State Railroad or the Denver & Rio Grande with their loud whistles and clanging bells, remind me of growing up in Beaumont, which was crisscrossed by five major rail lines. The clickety-clack when steel wheels crossed jointed steel rails and the station call of conductors followed by "All Aboard!" remind me of a happy time, even though it won't get me anywhere as fast as "Please fasten your seat belts and fix your seatback in the upright position for take-off."

People who lived in many small towns rarely had to consult a clock, because grist and sawmill whistles summoned

workers in the morning and indicated lunch time and quit-
ting time, not just for employees of the mill but for the whole
town. And dreaded were the short blast codes for fire or other
trouble at the mill or the mine.

Water pumps made sounds you just don't hear anymore.
First came the easy clang when you gave the handle its first
action to learn if the pump must be primed. Then the sound of
the water from a fruit jar saved for just that purpose, traveling
down to moisten and quicken the pump, and finally the sound
of the water coming up the pipe and into sink, bucket, or cup.
Other water-related sounds I remember include the squeal of
the pulley over a well as one drew up the precious—and
heavy—liquid, bucket by bucket. And the sound from Williams
Creek in the San Juan Mountains of southwest Colorado as
water sloshed with snowmelt rushing down to the Rio Grande.

More remembered sounds:

Al Sacker playing a giant organ in the Jefferson Theatre to
introduce the featured film.

The clinking of dominoes being shuffled before the draw
and slammed down in triumph when a trick was taken.

Daddy cranking the car on a cold morning and sometimes
having to bless it properly before the old Plymouth or Chevy
responded.

The peculiar grunt of pigs, that most intelligent of farm animals.

The creak of leather when swinging into a saddle.

Rain on a tin roof.

The power in the sound of a tractor.

The cry of my babies.

But the sounds I miss most are the voices. What wouldn't I give to hear Mother's voice just one more time?

Music

The Bard, or *some* old-timer, told us that music had the power to tame the savage beast, or something like that. Whoever told us that never sat in his car in traffic and felt his heart palpitate from the thump-thump-thump of the speaker system in a vehicle twenty feet away. Such noise does not tame; it enrages—at least it enrages me. Do I inflict Pavarotti or Beethoven on the uninterested? They probably would think the one a sports car and the other a Saint Bernard.

My progression in music—a reference that presumes "progress"—is the topic here. My earliest memories—late 1930s, early 1940s—are of my father playing guitar and singing "All Around The Water Tank" in imitation of Jimmy Rodgers, the Singing Brakeman, a.k.a. the founder of commercial country music. That is where I started in my musical progression—listening to my daddy sing, and with him, to Roy Acuff on the Grand Old Opry. Such music was called "hillbilly," a pejorative with malice aforethought.

That phase lasted until my high school years, when I thought Bill Haley invented rock'n'roll when I heard him and the Comets perform "Rock Around the Clock" in a movie. I knew not then of the pioneering role of Buddy Holly, though I knew much about The Big Bopper, of "Chantilly Lace" fame, who died with Buddy in the crash of their airplane. The "Bopper" was really J.P. Richardson, disk jockey for Radio KTRM in Beaumont, who played "easy listening from nine 'til midnight." We didn't even know J.P. could say "Hello, Baby," until the world knew.

I hoped the Beatles would go home to Liverpool and leave us alone, but have since changed my mind about them. The music of Lennon, McCartney, Harrison, and Starr, especially when played by full orchestra, reaches even crusty souls. But I have not altered my view of most other English imports or American imitators who confuse smoke, strobe lights, bare skin, and noise with music. And I shall ignore rap, hip-hop, or gangstra, or whatever. It is not music. I know this from one of the precious moments of grandparenthood that came close to feeling as good as revenge. Granddaughter Kelly wanted the car radio tuned to such music, and her father— himself a veteran of rock'n' roll, admonished her, "Kelly, that is *not* music." His mother and I collapsed.

With granddaughter Kelly.

In these autumn days of life, I have come to appreciate the music my mother wished for me a half century ago when she took me along to concerts of touring orchestras and opera performers. I did not understand it then, and still don't, but I can "feel" it now. It salves my soul. I do not embrace the "modern" composers much—someone playing a saw produces as pleasing sounds for me. But when Pavarotti reaches his high "C" or the oboe emerges again with the theme of "The New World," I stop whatever I am doing, as must have God on the seventh day, and marvel at the creation of it.

Shaving

One of the things that marks the age on me is that my lifetime spans the entire history of how men have shed their faces of the whiskers with which nature cursed us or blessed us, depending upon viewpoint. After all, no less a personage than Abraham Lincoln said that he grew a beard to hide his ugly features on the advice of a young girl. So perhaps some of us do the world a favor by hiding behind hirsute growth.

Maybe more of us *should* do that, but since I can't produce a decent looking beard anyway—and on behalf of domestic tranquility I don't want to—I join the great majority of males who invest five minutes a day in defying nature.

I started with a straight razor, which I happened to have because my first father, Archie McDonald, had been, among other professions before his death, a barber. Of course, I could have used a Case knife, because in those callow years I produced more fuzz than whiskers. These razors could be

Archie McDonald, my father, is the barber standing by the first chair on the left at barber school.

honed to a mighty fine edge, and if one gets off just a milli-angle or one's hand hitches a bit, the shaver can damage him-self. I recall losing a dime-sized hunk of epidermis to one of my father's razors.

My second father took a hand then, and instructed me in the somewhat safer safety razor by Gillette. This one looked like a "T" with a twisty part of the handle on the bottom that raised and lowered the top part to secure or release a thin, double-edged blade. When one side dulled, the shaver could simply turn the thing around and use the other side.

Next came the single-edge razor blade, which doubled as a great scraper of paint from glass because one side had *not* a sharpened edge that could be grasped and against which one could even apply pressure without danger of laceration except from the business side. Eventual sophistication of the single edge razor included twin and even triple cutting edges—one to "lift" and one to "cut" and I suppose one to spare—with the whole head of the thing attached and detached pretty much without touching the cutting part of the instrument at all. After that, Bic and others contributed disposable razors to our throwaway society.

Best of all, however, are electric shavers. Norelco, Remington, Braun, and others market a device that will take an electrical charge sufficient to provide powered shaving for about a week—a little longer if one doesn't go for the smoothest of shaves. It is nigh impossible to cut yourself with one of these things unless a gap appears in the shaving screen, unlike the so-called safety razor, which can still produce life-threatening wounds if applied with malice.

And for all this effort, what do we get? Well, there is that domestic tranquility we cited earlier. Apart from that, maybe Abe's little friend knew best.

Cars I've Known

My first car was a Ford sedan, about 1949 vintage, awarded to me in 1954 when Halliburton Oil Well Cementing Company transferred my father from Beaumont to Lake Charles, and I enrolled at Lamar Tech. I received the car because I was the only member of the family left in Beaumont who could drive, and Aunt Vennie and Aunt Jonnie needed transportation.

My second auto was a green Plymouth sedan previously driven by my folks. In it I courted Judy. We called it the "hummingbird" because she told me she intended to become an "old maid junior high math teacher and drive a red Thunderbird." Part of that ambition yet lives, I am afraid.

When we moved to Baton Rouge and LSU, we drove a yellow-and-white 1955 Chevy, and thought ourselves quite racy in it. The Chevy was succeeded by a Comet, one of Mercury's mistakes, and mine, too, because it was, without exception, the hottest car to drive I ever saw. I mean "hot" as in temperature.

*Judy, our son Tucker, and Aunt Jonnie with our first new car,
a Rambler.*

When we moved to Murray, Kentucky, in 1963 for me to begin teaching, we rode in a Rambler, the first new car and first car with a factory installed air-conditioner that we owned. Previously, but not in the Comet, we had an under-dash mounted air cooler, never very efficient. Mostly, we used the "four-sixty" cooling system—roll down all four windows and drive sixty miles an hour.

That Rambler cooled us down. I remember driving beside the Mississippi River in August, ninety-nine degrees and rising, and Judy sleeping under a blanket. I tell you, A/C was the harbinger of Heaven for Southerners.

We drove that old Rambler to Nacogdoches in 1964, and then for another decade, and I wish I had it still. It was succeeded by a station wagon, a Chrysler Fifth Avenue, and a series of vans, all of which have been serviceable, at least most of the time.

Maturity, or call it callousness, has robbed me of romanticism about most of these vehicles. One goes and one comes, tools of the necessity to travel. But I wish that old Rambler could take me home again. I'd park it right beside that red Thunderbird.

Manners

People ask my opinion about the "younger generation." Because I work perpetually with eighteen-year-old college freshmen to "senior" twenty-two-year olds, I suppose that makes me an expert on such issues—at least in the view of my questioners. What they want to know about is the behavior of today's college students, at least in class, and if they are as prepared for college as in the past. Here are some thoughts on modern manners.

Today's college students are not as well dressed as were their parents and grandparents. When I began teaching, some boys wore blue jeans, but the girls never did. Unless actually in a gym class or in their dormitory, girls *never* wore shorts and rarely wore slacks. It was always skirts-with-blouses or dresses, with flat shoes. Both genders always wore sleeves. Now, a female college student in hose-and-heels is identified as a senior with a job interview scheduled for that day. Even in their jeans, guys wore pressed shirts that actually buttoned up the front. Now, jeans are unisex and worn primarily in winter. Otherwise, the standard uniform is a T-shirt that advertises beer or Tommy Hilfiger, shorts, and shower sandals that flip-flop with every step. Men and women wear this. Score one for the old-timers.

Then there is hair. Forty years ago the guys cut theirs into flattops and the gals brushed and "set" their glory in flowing waves. Then came the 1960s and 1970s, when men's hair reached their shoulders and women's reached their *gluteus maximuses*, parted in the middle and straight down, in accordance with some law. They have since fazed through a fashion that dictated curly strands that looked perpetually wet and in need of a good brushing. Since we seem to have overcome that, praise God, score one for the kids.

A word about caps—the "gimme" variety with the adjustable strap. Girls and guys wear these to, in, and through class, and I have given up asking that they remove them since the weather in class probably won't change. It just got to be too much of a hassle. I expect that a student who did that thirty years ago would have been dismissed from class, possibly from college. Old-timers win again.

But on the actual question of manners, eighteen- to twenty-two-year-olds are pretty much the same, then and now. I don't recall all that much thirsting after scholarship from the parents of modern students. So I'll call the comparison a draw and hope today's crop will be as productive as their predecessors.

Gardening

In spring we who bear the curse of Cain stir from winter's sloth and get ready to break ground for another season of gardening. Part of that sloth involves investigating catalogues for seeds and sets appropriate to our season and clime. This sloth includeth coveting overpriced and fancy rototillers and other tools, each guaranteed by sworn testimony to ease pain in the back, double production, chase away pests, and make us the envy of the neighborhood. Then we putteth away childish things and approach the patch of earth that is our curse and our blessing.

I have been gardening a long time. I need to point out that I mean vegetable gardening; only lately has Judy enlisted me in the culture of plants that bloom without leaving something to eat behind.

My first was a "victory" garden, c. 1944. My father hired a man and his mule to plow up our entire back yard, say fifty-by-fifty feet, so we could enjoy "fresh" vegetables even if there

Yield of the garden.

was a war on. Since Dad worked double shifts at the shipyard, guess who got to water and weed. Well, to tell the truth, it was my Mother, but I helped. Some.

During graduate school at LSU, Judy and I planted corn, greens, and okra in the back yard. Anyone can grow okra in Baton Rouge. The greens were good, too, but a neighbor's kid pulled up *all* the corn after watching me thin it. Looked like fun, he said. Fences are essential for good gardening.

I started in again a few years after we became homeowners. A neighbor, Tex Spurlock, loaned me his rototiller and together we hauled organic matter to work into my sand hill soil. Over the years I tilled in about five tons of organic matter—sawdust, eight gazillion leaves, and the contributions of contented cows—and eight inches down it is still sand. But that eight inches has produced trillions of tomatoes—I always plant enough to make friends—the sweetest corn imaginable, Louisiana Purple Pod beans, onions, peppers, and squash. Don't plant zucchini unless you really like it because it will reach the size of a baseball bat if you don't harvest it soon enough.

Nothing beats the taste of truly "fresh" vegetables—a vine ripened tomato or corn boiled within thirty minutes of leaving the stalk are different vegetables than those bought in stores, even if they look alike.

But this is gourmet stuff, not thrift. Figuring in the cost of the tiller, city water, and time, those tomatoes cost about $5 a pound.

Vacation Bible School

For a kid, the last day of school is a thing of joy. This is more social suggestion than a genuine feeling of relief, at least for elementary school scholars who mostly like school and their schoolmates. Still, every year I see youngsters on the news who swarm out of the school as if they had just been released from a dentist's chair. I think they stage these escapes for the benefit of TV camera operators who wish they could have the summer off from work. Within days, kids across America will be complaining, "there's nothing to do."

Back in time a ways, there was. It was called Vacation Bible School, and every church in town promoted these summertime, weeklong, activity-filled enterprises that occupied youth just fine. We didn't know that the Baptist, Methodist, and Church of God preachers even talked to each other, but they must have because their churches held VBS in *succession*, not in competition.

This was a wonderful conspiracy. Each congregation welcomed us all, and I don't recall any high-pressure denominational proselytizing. All, however, were intent on saving our souls and keeping the devil's workshop at bay by occupying as much of our summertime as possible.

I was introduced to the world of Vacation Bible School in Burkeville, a sawmill community located in Newton County, Texas. I spent a week with Aunt Thelma and Uncle Bill and my cousins Eleanor Lois and Kathryn. Just how it worked out that I would visit the very week the Baptists held Vacation Bible School, I do not know, but probably there was more conspiracy involved.

We walked to the church each morning for assembly. We had Bible drills, a contest to see who could locate a particular verse first. We sang hymns, the good ones that everyone knew. We had craft lessons—I remember making a sharp pair of bookends by splitting a section of oak limb, nailing boards on the bottom of one end of each half, and shellacking them to a fine luster. And, of course, we had cookies and punch with a sandwich lunch.

I had so much fun getting the devil chased out of me that I stayed on for the Methodist and Church of God versions. I even got to sing in a quartet at the Church of God after I learned to read shape notes. I can still identify the notes from their location on the staff, but I have forgotten what the shapes mean.

For a few years afterward my summer visits to Burkeville were timed by my elders to coincide with Vacation Bible Schools. I am the better for it. I expect that I learned something about the Bible. I know I learned to love to sing, how to make bookends, and a lot about ecumenism.

I hope rural churches still do this. We need to learn, somewhere, that Methodists don't really have horns, no matter what Aunt Thelma said.

The Renegade Church

My wife and I have attended some pretty memorable churches. In Rome, we attended Mass in St. Peters. The Pope was there, too. We sat in the choir during Evensong in St. Paul's in London, heard chants in Canterbury Cathedral and in St. Francis's own church in Assisi, marveled at a Mozart concert in an ancient house of worship in the Buda half of Budapest. Not bad for a Baptist.

I wasn't always a Baptist. I started out in another direction, then married a Baptist—you know the rest. Even so, we are pretty ecumenical when it comes to churchgoing, and so we have visited mosques, temples, and brush arbors during lives punctuated by weddings, funerals, baptisms, and confirmations in faiths not entirely our own. We are the richer for searching for the Spirit in disparate venues, but enriched most of all by the churches we have called our own.

There was Southside in Baton Rouge, where the Rev. Troy Hargis and I hoped he washed away my transgressions and where I got to know a great LSU football player named Jim Taylor. Then came First Baptist in Murray, Kentucky, site of my first teaching assignment, where repetition convinced me that "Amazing Grace" was the greatest of all hymns.

We moved to Nacogdoches in 1964 and affiliated again with a First Baptist, partially because its nursery gave our eighteen-month-old some playmates. Then, in 1968, we were one of five families who began a fellowship named Austin Heights Baptist Church. Often I have called it a renegade church because we seem perpetually out of step with others in our denomination on civil and gender rights and such issues as inerrancy. However, I don't want to dwell on that here.

What I do want to say about Austin Heights—which still lets me be its resident and designated sinner even though I sometimes go to Mass with the Pope—and about other churches like it in every denomination, is that it is filled with folks who know when you are sick and care when you die. They really do house the homeless, feed the hungry, heal the sick, clothe the naked, and visit those in jail.

Austin Heights is never likely to amount to much as the world judges churches. It isn't distinguished in architecture, has no TV ministry, is not pressed to buy adjacent property for parking lots. Good for churches with those opportunities and problems, but I don't miss them. What does awe me about the place is that they let even me, and the Pope if he showed up, come in. I'll bet St. Francis could even bring his birds and squirrels.

Favorite Hymns

Roger Paynter, a preacher friend who I helped raise when he did his practice preaching at our little renegade Baptist church, has gone on to the big time. But he keeps us on the mailing list of church publications wherever he goes. A recent edition included a list of the "Top 10" Baptist hymns.

It shouldn't surprise anyone that Baptists rank "Amazing Grace" Number One with them and with the Lord, followed, in order, by "How Great Thou Art," "Because He Lives," "The Old Rugged Cross," "Victory In Jesus," "Holy, Holy, Holy," "Great Is Thy Faithfulness," "Blessed Assurance," "To God Be The Glory," and, at Number Ten, "It is Well With My Soul." I would put that last one as Number Two.

The late Lewis Grizzard oft expressed preference for "Precious Memories" and requested it be sung at his send-off, and I believe that it was.

I like all these hymns, of course, but two of them are precious indeed to my ear:

I'm almost petulant that "Amazing Grace" has achieved pop status in the culture. That lessens it some for me, as selfish as that sounds, because all other wretches may find just as much solace in being "found." Do most of them know that the writer, the trusty self-identified wretch John Newton, was celebrating a grace so broad and deep as to extend even to a transporter of slaves from Africa?

"It Is Well With My Soul" is less well known, but its origin is also compelling. The writer of those words, Horatio Spafford, composed them at sea while sailing past the site on the Atlantic Ocean where his four daughters had perished during an earlier voyage. Its message is contained in these lyrics: "Whatever my lot, thou hast taught me to say, it is well, it is well, with my soul."

These hymns hold poignancy for me. When we helped to start that little renegade church, I suppose I was the most wretched of the bunch and so identified with the message of "Amazing Grace" that I requested it be sung almost every week. In time, that little Baptist Church in the hollow became almost as well known as the "Amazing Grace Church" as by its actual name.

And the other hymn? In times of stress in our lives, "It Is Well With My Soul" seems to pop up in the order of worship just at the right time to remind us that no matter how the things that worry us turn out, we have staked our lives on a higher authority than ourselves.

For the wretches of this world, that is powerful medicine.

Favorite Books

Our town's newspaper contains a weekly feature, a "Personal Profile" of some local newsmaker such as the United Way drive chairman or the rodeo parade organizer. Their profile always discloses that the Bible is their favorite book. This happens so often that I have concluded that I live in the most pious place in America.

Now, I come from a long line of Bible readers, and I think my wife has read the whole book at least twice in a daily regimen prescribed by *The One Year Bible* people. I can't make *that* claim, though I am familiar with the Scriptures, especially the ones I memorized to please my Sunday school teachers. I *like* the Bible, and rely upon its messages, but, truth be told, I won't represent it to you as my favorite book.

I have several favorite books, in no particular order:

Dr. Suess' *Green Eggs and Ham*, with *Fox in Socks* a close competitor, because I read them half a gazillion times to our kids, at bedtime, I think until they graduated from junior high school. The power is not in the plots, but in the memory of doing that.

John R. Tunis's *The Kid from Tomkinsville*, about a baseball player with a rural background who made it to the Big Leagues, something I wanted to do about the time I read Tunis's books.

Will James's *Smokey, Sand*, and other first-person presentations of the cowboy life, when, of course, cowboying constituted my calling.

Margaret Mitchell's *Gone With The Wind*, which I have subtitled "a social history of antebellum northern Georgia" when permitting students to read it for credit in my Civil War course, because its history is accurate and it created Southern stereotypes for several generations after its publication in the 1930s.

Mickey Spillane's *I, The Jury*, because I read it with prurient interest just as my own sap was rising, and for a while I embraced the whole *noire* concept, whether filmed or printed.

Two or three of Jim Michener's novels, probably *Texas*—because he listed me in the credits—or *Centennial*, belong on this list, as does the seventh grade textbook I helped write, which I hope is selling splendidly.

Oh, and I don't want to forget the Bible. That belongs on my list, too, though I don't read it as often as I should.

A friend who loved to read—the wife of a very wealthy man—once asked me what book she ought to have placed in her casket with her. Without hesitation, I advised taking her husband's checkbook. I'll have to say that tickled *her* a lot more than *him*.

House Calls

The other day I called Leonard, the plumber who unstops sinks and things, to address a rather acute problem of drainage. When one is not a handyman, one depends on the promptness, not to mention the reasonableness, of kind souls who come into your home to make things right again.

I started thinking about the number of folks who have entré to our home, often when we are not there, and concluded that—so far—all have been a remarkably cheerful and honest lot—at least once one accepts the reality that few service persons will darken your door without a fee of $50 or more just to show up, with charges beyond that for what they must repair.

About the only exceptions to that rule are regular providers of lawn or cleaning service. I suppose such things are built into whatever you have agreed to pay for the service.

Others who keep our place operational are the air condition/heating unit repairman, the exterminator who checks for termites and chases away other pestilence—and Leonard, of course.

The house in which I grew up had many more callers than these.

Let's start with the doctor. If you were too ill to travel, a real medical doctor would come to your home. He carried a bag filled with nostrums and instruments, and usually he administered the first dosage and left a prescription for whatever additional medication was required. As often, the doctor provided confidence that you would survive. Now, it is "go to the emergency room." Surely they are better equipped to deal with what ails you, assuming you survive to arrive at the hospital, but the process is less pleasing.

Insurance representatives called monthly, and even weekly, to collect premiums, especially life or burial insurance. It was standard practice in the 1930s to buy a $1,000 life insurance policy on the new-born, and the salesman who came to your home to sell it returned to collect premiums. The salesman marked the transaction in a small receipt book kept in the home, and in a much larger binder containing the records of all the company's clients that salesman served.

The home-delivery milkman visited nearly every home. You put out empty bottles on the doorstep early on delivery day—two or three times each week—and the next time you looked out, there would be bottles filled with milk. Better get it in the "ice box" quickly, lest it spoil.

The milk drop doubled in homes also on the route of the diaper service. Yes, in the old days, babes wore white cotton cloth diapers that had to be washed. God bless the service that did this, then returned weekly with fresh, cleaned diapers. I disposed of only one of these—when I lost my grip while emptying my son's soiled diaper in the commode.

Where was Leonard when I needed him then?

Water Witching

Ever watch a water-witch work?

If you have not, let me tell you—it is spooky. This experience has come my way dozens of times and I don't know yet if I believe. It *seems* to work for those who have the "gift."

Let's examine the parts of their label. The first part (water) means they are searching for subterranean pools of water. The second part (witch) suggests a supernatural—not exactly sinister or evil, but somehow "not natural"—route to achieving that goal. Maybe it is that second part that makes us wary, and that is unfortunate.

Most of my observing of this phenomenon was performed by a wonderful gentleman named Bert Barrett who let me marry his even more wonderful daughter. The family alerted me to this unique skill long after the ink had dried on the marriage certificate, so I took it in stride.

Bert needed to locate the best place to attempt a water well on land in Newton County, Texas, where he was building a weekend retreat. He cut a forked stick, with inward slopes on the cut for thumb comfort. Only a fresh cut will do, of course; you would not expect a dry stick to find water. Bert grasped the ends of the fork and rotated his wrists so the pointed end of the "y" angled up in front about forty-five degrees from level. He walked back and forth several times in a pre-selected area whose surface signs appeared promising.

Occasionally the stick would dip downward. After the stick had repeated its bow several times at the same spot, approached from different directions, he had identified the drill site. And, by golly, there was water waiting.

I have seen Bert find lost jewelry and other articles with the same—dare I say miraculous?—technique. An even greater phenomenon was directing his son where to dig a water well in Colorado as he "witched" a map of the area while in *Beaumont, Texas*. Even if we believe the stick is attracted to water, as might have been the case in Newton County where witcher, water, and wand were in close proximity, one must wonder how this worked over a distance of 1,000 miles.

Bert has directed the drilling sites for scores of water wells and has "found" oil, but I cannot report that anyone drilled for black gold under his direction. Maybe they lacked the capital. Or the nerve. I do know that others have found oil that way. A few years ago a graduate student told me that her father, a pioneer of the EasTex Oil Field, attributed some of his early success to "dousing." That is the term used in the oil patch. With geologists and seismologists afoot, few oilmen but old-time wildcatters will admit foreswearing science for twitches in a twig as a route to riches.

Bert Barrett and his forked stick, looking for water in Newton County.

Another form of the witcher's art I have observed involved welding rods. This seems to work best in locating underground water or natural gas lines. The operator bends the end of two rods to approximate a pistol grip. The same walking about follows, with the rods held parallel. When they cross into an "X" you have found the line. One suspects some electrical field provides the energy for the movement.

I do not claim the gift, only an interest. Once I did present a paper on this subject as an after-dinner talk. The room was filled with skeptics, of course. I reported first-hand testimony of the converted and rebuttals from non-believers. Came then the time to grasp the stick, as I had seen Bert do it. I held it to the side of the podium . . . and we all watched the stick descend until it pointed straight down into a glass of water.

I don't know why they wouldn't believe me. They were all Baptists. That, and marrying Bert's daughter, is how I became a Baptist, too—believing in something I cannot prove.

Remembering That Year

At a fiftieth high school reunion, I found myself remembering that magical year we bid goodbye to high school and many friends from the Class of 1954. Maybe you're old enough to remember, too.

"I Love Lucy," "Dragnet," and "Ed Sullivan's Toast of the Town" dominated primetime television, but newcomers "Father Knows Best," "The Loretta Young Show," and "Stop The Music" with Bert Parks showed promise. Emmy awards went to the "U.S. Steel Hour" for drama and to Danny Thomas of "Make Room For Daddy" as best actor and Loretta Young as best actress.

We attended the Jefferson or Liberty theatres to see new movies "On The Waterfront," which won the Academy Award as best picture of the year, and "The Country Girl" and "Sabrina" with Grace Kelly and Audrey Hepburn in the title roles, though John Wayne topped all Hollywood actors in popularity and the even more important category of ticket sales.

We listened to popular recordings—78s and 45s— "Three Coins In The Fountain," "Teach Me Tonight," and "Shake, Rattle, and Roll."

Broadway fare, which we would not get to see until road shows arrived years later, included "The Caine Mutiny Court Martial" and "Witness for The Prosecution" and musicals "The Pajama Game" and "Peter Pan."

In medicine, more than 900,000 children received Dr. Jonas Salk's vaccine against polio. In science, Boeing tested its new jet, the 707, the Navy launched the *Nautilis*, its first atomic-powered submarine, and Linus Pauling won the Nobel Prize in chemistry.

The Giants won the World Series and Willie Mays was MVP of the National League. The Ohio State Buckeyes were the national champs in college football, but Alan Ameche of Wisconsin won the Heisman.

The words "under God" were added to the Pledge of Allegiance. Senator Joseph McCarthy split his britches in televised hearings over his allegation of communist influence in the U.S. Army. Phrases such as "massive retaliation," "windfall profits," "fall out," and "do-it-yourself" entered our lexicon.

Was that *really* fifty years ago?

Festivals and Fairs

Fairs originated in medieval times. I know this because of that great song from the musical "Camelot" about escorting Lady Guinevere to the fair. And throughout American history county and state fairs have been staged as exhibitions of agricultural and domestic skills and as arenas for fun and competition in rural areas, usually held in the summer and fall.

Festivals, on the other hand, are creatures of Chambers of Commerce. Local leaders take inventory of what distinguishes them and set out to celebrate that very thing. It doesn't matter what it is—sunflowers, black-eyed peas, blueberries, even fire ants will do. The most important question is: can we convince people to bring money and buy a T-shirt?

Both events are about money, of course, and festivals really aren't more commercial than fairs. They are just younger. Here are some thoughts about each.

I have been a participant in our community's Heritage Festival for more than twenty years. This one started out nobly—to raise funds for the preservation of our Chamber's deteriorating headquarters building, and for other such projects if there was any money left over. Heralds buy the privilege of voting annually on who shall be the queen of the festival, and there is much eating and partying. My contribution is to write clues based on local history that will lead the quick and the determined to the Heritage Festival "treasure"—a piece of paper worth $200. What has impressed me most about this is the number of people who search for the thing. Most don't need the money—they just respond to the challenge. I like that.

About fairs. I haven't attended one in a long time, but none could equal in my mind the South East Texas State Fair in Beaumont in 1951 when my Uncle George let me show a Hereford calf in the livestock competition. I had to join the 4-H Club to qualify, but they were lax and didn't make me attend meetings. What I did was bond with that dumb calf. He taught me how to lead him around the show ring, not to stand within range of his hind foot—which kicks *forward*— and to try to look nonchalant when his body eliminated wastes in public places.

I survived, finishing eleventh in a field of thirty or so competitors. That blamed steer sold for about $1,000—and this was more than a half century ago. There were other benefits: I skipped school a lot during fair week—to care for the calf, don't you know—with permission from the ag teacher.

And this: I was introduced to the wonders of human female anatomy. I was about fifteen years old and bestirred by the natural hormonal revolution of adolescence. So some of us underagers broke the law and attended a tent show that featured "Evelyn West and Her Million Dollar Chest," and Evelyn educated us about why King Arthur's knights all wanted to take Guinevere to the fair.

I have always believed that fairs offer a variety of educational opportunities.

Little League Baseball

By mid-April, the Little League baseball season is about half done in the South. I see practices starting in February so I assume actual play begins in March. An early finish is required so playing seasons come out about even with the school year.

Seeing those bantam infielders and outfielders takes me back to the late 1940s when I held down first base on a team that played in a juvenile league in Beaumont. We had never even heard of the national Little League movement; ours was really more akin to old-time sandlot or pickup games because the lineup varied.

The players included my friends Bill and Dick Spillar, who lived around the corner. Bill was our "manager," a term we copied from the real baseball operations we followed closely. Jimmy Craig, Freddie Lender, and a few others made up the team. I don't recall our won-loss record, which may be one of the blessings of maturity.

Seeing those youngsters also kindled memories of my coaching days when Tucker and Chris—three years apart— were members of the RoadRunners, one of a great many teams in the far more structured competition in the 1970s. I had agreed to help a fellow named Ben coach the boys, then Ben backed out and left me and Wendell Dickerson holding the ball, as it were.

None of this makes me an expert on anything, but per- haps does justify these opinions: Little League baseball is a wholesome enough activity as long as parents don't impose their own competitiveness vicariously through their progeny. The physical and mental exercise of the game, its environ- ment, and perhaps challenging one's self to hit better, run faster, and field balls more efficiently have positive benefits so long as fulfilling Dad's—or even Mom's—ego expectation is not the primary object.

Little League can leave some scars, and I don't mean just physical ones. I recall a youngster on another team who had to sit out a playoff game because he violated his coach's rule against missing practices to participate in another family activity. Small boys are not professional players on whom such demands may be made legitimately. When you pay a person to perform, you can set such rules. A volunteer coach of twelve-year-olds should find better ways to encourage dependability.

I think the point of this is to remember that Little League is a good time to allow kids to be kids, which is helped quite a bit when adults behave like adults.

Summer Evenings

The other evening Judy and I sat on the patio enjoying the end of the day. The sun long had disappeared behind a bank of pines, and only cardinals and a pair of doves, both late diners among our winged friends, still visited Judy's feeders. Our back yard is fenced, a relic of child and dog rearing days, but we still like the sense of privacy the barrier creates, even if that mostly is illusion.

Sounds of children playing some game or the other came over the fence. They remained unseen, but their exuberance, their delight, took us back to similar scenes in the 1940s when *we* squealed and ran and jumped to burn excessive energy of youth. We slept better then, tired from spending our joy on the chase, the game, the moment, not worrying about what to wear the next day, tensions of the workplace or the world, or relationships.

Remember Sheldon Harnick's words from "Fiddler On The Roof," "Is this the little girl I carried? Is this the little boy at play? When did she get to be a beauty? When did he grow to be so tall? I don't remember growing older. When did they?"

That is a reverie, is it not? Of halcyon days filled with playing "soldier" during World War II; jumping off Tommy Lender's washhouse roof with a towel around my neck for a cape, attached by a safety pin, imagining I was Superman "leaping tall buildings." Later on, it might have been baseball, just two-handed catch or a pickup game with the Spillar kids and a few others, when you started in right field and worked your way to bat, one position and one out at a time.

Lots of living was done in those precious hours after suppertime. Our houses were not air-conditioned then, so we savored the cooling of the air with the daily demise of the sun, and this miracle worked so much faster outside than inside our houses. Even as it grew darker, we continued to postpone surrender of the day, and, cleaning done, grownups might come out to sit on the porch and visit. We watched moths and other night bugs buzz around the street light on the corner, scrutinized cars that passed by to see who could identify the make, model, and year, planned activities for the next day. At last, tired, sometimes cranky, we gave up the vigil, bathed, and hoped the attic or window fan would cool us enough to sleep. Somehow, it always did.

With apologizes to Mr. Harnick for a few changes in his words, doesn't this sum it well? "Sunrise, Sunset, Sunrise, Sunset, When did she get to be a beauty? When did [I] grow to be so tall? Wasn't it yesterday when [we] were small? Swiftly fly the years, One season following another, Laden with happiness and tears."

Play on through the twilight; long is the night.

Family Vacations

Where are you going on vacation this summer? In the working class world in which I grew up, economic circumstance generally determined the answer to that question, and that usually meant visiting relatives who did not charge motel rates.

My father worked as a milk route salesman until he found a home at Halliburton, now an international conglomerate but then a family-oriented business mostly concerned with oil field services. Milk trucks and cement trucks take one to warm work, so come mid-summer Daddy mostly wanted to go where it was cooler. So we might drive to Hot Springs, Arkansas, that's about 450 miles, which wasn't a bit cooler than Beaumont, but at least it had hills around it. He took the baths to relieve an aching back and we might visit the auctions for which the resort city was once famous, but I don't recall us ever buying anything.

We also visited relatives in New Madrid County, Missouri. It wasn't any cooler there, either, but the room and board were free. We might stay three days, at the most.

Our method of to-ing and from-ing was in the family car—as in our *only* car—and we felt lucky to have it. A succession of Fords and Plymouths—all two-seaters—managed to hold Daddy, Mother, siblings George, Nancy, and later baby John, plus me, of course.

Whatever the destination, we drove straight through. The air-conditioning method was known as "four-sixty"—four windows down and sixty miles per hour, the maximum speed then allowed by law. That wasn't much cooler, either, but it was sure windy and noisy.

Games helped pass the long hours. Careful records were kept on the duration of the trip—thirteen hours one year set the mark to be beaten next year—and gas mileage was calculated with each fill-up. We looked for license plates from as many states as possible, and the first one who shouted that Burma Shave signs were coming up captured an audience for this effective advertising. Everyone helped the driver look out for highway patrolmen, not that we did much speeding. If one did so, in those days before coolants, you were apt to need to add water to the radiator.

We never stopped at hotels or motels unless there was car trouble, and the first meal of the trip came from home with us; if we consumed more food, it was likely lunch meat and bread, maybe washed down with a Coke purchased at a small grocery located near the highway. What I shall delicately call "pit stops" were achieved behind a tree since there were no state-maintained rest stops and good manners kept us from asking to use the bathroom in a gas station or store unless we planned to make a purchase there.

Looking back, all this seems much more exhausting than a vacation ought to be, and it was not a bit cooler behind that tree, either.

Starting School
in August

Somewhere in Deuteronomy it must say, "Thou shalt not commence the teaching of thy young in the heat of summer; nay, wait until after Labor Day, when thy land cools a bit, to instruct thy young." Apparently modern educationists and lawmakers are not as familiar with the Scriptures as they should be, for verily, we "commence" school now in the dog days of August.

Time was, back when Moses and I attended Averill Elementary and on through French High School in Beaumont, the Labor Day Commandment commanded obedience. We left off the schooling in the Spring long about baseball season and enjoyed a long, leisurely summer of pickup games, a week or so with one or more sets of grandparents or aunts and uncles, attended whatever Vacation Bible School might be in session. Teachers scattered to recuperate.

We thought little of school in those halcyon days, save pity for those who had flunked something and had to attend summer school so they could remain in the same grade with their friends. And we never, ever, returned to class until after Labor Day. We were not Tom, Huck, and Becky, exactly, but our "good ol' summertimes" were sacred.

This civilizing schedule continued for me through high school, college, even graduate school. One good argument for it back then was that none of the schools were air-conditioned and it was cruel to corral our squirming masses into classroom ovens—though this never prohibited us from outdoor activities in the July and August sun.

Then educationists and lawmakers found alarm in declining classroom performance, and, I expect, sought remedy by stretching the process. So we have the appearance of improvement in the lengthening of the school year, though contact hours between teachers and students remain about the same what with all the new holidays, spring/winter/fall breaks, teacher work days, early release, and what have you.

The impact is substantial. We used to have a nine-month school year, leaving plenty of time for summer play and paying the piper by summer-school clients. Now it is a ten-month proposition. Elementary and secondary teachers attend year-beginning orientation sessions during the first week of August and their scholars fall in a week or so later. Even in university, we begin faculty meetings in mid-August. I am not sure we are creating more than an illusion of better education with an imaginary longer year.

One advantage is that this early start allows completion of the fall semester prior to Christmas, instead of having a two-week layover into January. It also leaves our facilities fallow for nearly a month in December-January, sometimes half that in May, and weeks at a time during semesters. But I am not certain the yield is improved, and I wonder if we ought to mess with Deuteronomy this way.

Houses and Homes

If you are of sufficient age, you might remember popular poet Edgar Guest's observation that "It takes a heap of livin' to make a house a home." Literature and popular culture are filled with illustrations about the differences between the two, with the general conclusion that an humble dwelling where love abounds beats the greatest mansion where it does not.

This reverie grows from the move that the Boss and I made last year to what likely will be our *last* home, assuming we escape the assisted living/nursing facilities that await so many now at the end of their days.

It strikes me that a succession of living places is a pretty good framework for a person's biography. So here is mine:

I was born in Beaumont, Texas. Mother and I rode home from St. Theresa Hospital, which I suppose was my first early abode, to 2015 Liberty Street, where we lived with Mother's mother, sister, and great aunt. There I passed elementary

Our house at 2015 Liberty Street, Beaumont, taken during the city's once-a-decade snowfall.

years, the death of my father at age eight, and Mother's remarriage to George Tucker. We moved next door to 2009 Liberty Street, which was handy because I could compare supper menus and choose which suited me best.

Then we moved north to 2389 Wilson Street, where we lived until I was a senior in French High School. Daddy Tucker was transferred to Lake Charles then, so I moved back in with my aunts at 2015 Liberty to finish high school, then college.

In my senior year at Lamar—1957—Judy Barrett plighted her troth with mine and we set up shop in a quadruplex at 1427 Orange Avenue. That September, we moved into a garage apartment at 5512 Mercer Street in Houston so I could attend graduate school at the Rice Institute. The second year we lived at 4233 Albans Road. Rice gave me a master's degree in 1960 and passed us off to LSU, in Baton Rouge, where we lived three years in World War II-era housing at 3802 Sweetbriar Street and where we hatched our first son. Then came a new brick rental in Murray, Kentucky, at 306 Broach Street.

A year later—we are up to 1964—we moved to 921 Durst Street in Nacógdoches because Stephen F. Austin State College, now University, let me work there—for the past four decades and counting. In 1966, pregnant again, we built the house at 1615 Redbud, where we reared our two boys, various dogs and cats—most of which are buried on the premises (the dogs and cats, not the boys)—about thirty-five great vegetable gardens, and made lots of memories.

What surprises me most, having forgotten so much that transpired over all these decades, is that I still remember all those addresses.

Moving a Cat

Of all the problems associated with moving from our residence of thirty-seven years to a new-for-us home by the creek, the one that troubled Judy most was how our overprivileged cat would make the move.

GG—short for Grey Ghost, which tells you his color and personality simultaneously—came into our lives a decade or so ago when Judy took our previous feline, Alison, to the vet and came home with two of the critters. GG was misadvertised. The sign said "Free Cat—And He's Sweet." All kittens are sweet, of course, but they grow out of it. GG's arrival did not please Alison, so she disappeared—along with *his* sweetness.

Now the lone critter among us, GG became the one cat of my acquaintance who refused to take to the litter box. He much preferred to litter the bathtub or a dark corner of the guest bathroom, but vigilance in keeping such doors closed did more to improve that situation than GG's adaptability to modern, indoor feline waste disposal.

Our cat, GG

GG trained us when he wanted to go outside to stalk the wild lizards and birds he rarely, but still too often, caught. He would crouch on the window near the back door. This did not mean that he actually would exit by that door, for darkness, rain, or plain cussedness sometimes would cause him to go to the garage door—once you had opened the back door. A desire to reenter was signaled by further shredding of patio window screens near the door—unless the hunt was successful. Then he would yowl through clenched teeth and if we forgot the meaning of this, GG marched in with a mouse or a lizard trophy to present to Judy.

You might ask, why would I want to move a tyrant with such bad manners? If I had the opportunity to lie here I would say that I didn't want to move him, that this was just one of the concessions one makes to keep a spouse happy. There is some truth in that, for I do want to keep her happy. But I am a little fond of GG myself, though I would never confess that to Judy.

Our move took us to the creek bottom where hawks and owls and probably coyotes earn their living the hard way. Friends warned that our mighty hunter would become the huntee in his new habitat. Such predictions so disturbed Judy that she determined then to make GG an indoor cat. She wrapped him in an afghan for the short trip to our new home, then she and our friend Angela watched as GG explored the new surroundings until he found the closet, where he hid under my hanging suits for the next two days. Then he came out and used the litter box.

Maybe that dumb cat had been living in the wrong house for the past decade.

Older Than Dirt

A former student—now a college professor herself and therefore old enough to know better—sent me a test of age. It began with non-evaluated teasers, such as did I remember headlight dimmer switches on the car's floor, *real* ice boxes, or giving arm signals to indicate right or left turns or stopping to other drivers.

Then this nasty thing got down to specifics with a list of twenty-five "do you remembers:"

—Blackjack chewing gum.

—Little wax Coca-Cola bottles with colored sugar water inside.

—Candy cigarettes.

—Soda pop machines that dispensed bottles.

—Coffee shops with tableside jukeboxes.

—Home milk delivery in glass bottles with card-board stoppers.

—Party lines (for telephone service).

—Newsreels before movies.

—P.F. Flyers.

—Butch wax.

—Telephone numbers with a word prefix.

—Pea-shooters.

—Howdy Doody.

—45 rpm records.

—S&H Green Stamps.

—Hi-Fi's.

—Metal ice trays with a lever.

—Mimeograph paper.

—Blue flashbulbs.

—Packards.

—Roller skate keys.

—Cork popguns.

—Drive-in movies.

—Studebakers.

—And, number twenty-five—wash tub wringers.

According to the rules, if you remember five or less, you are still young; six to ten, you are maturing; eleven to fifteen, "don't tell your age;" and if you remember sixteen or more, you are older than dirt.

Well, not only am I familiar with all twenty-five of these "remembers," I have had personal contact with most of them. And I could throw in a few more, such as Grapettes, Brownie cameras, and plastic pocket savers.

Now that I have been certified, at least by this evaluation instrument, "older than dirt," I more than understand an old professor named Walter Prescott Webb, who conceived the Great Frontier theory. In a nutshell, Webb argued that the discovery of the New World provided the Old World—or Europe—with a frontier filled with new land, lots of things, but not many more people, and this fostered a 400-year economic boom. But, said Webb, by 1930, all available land, the things it produced, and the number of people those things could support, was again in the same ratio as they were in 1500. In other words, the boom was over; afterwards we just argue about shares of the same finite wealth. Boy, that seemed pessimistic.

On the other hand, Webb, a widower, remarried when he was seventy-two years old. If that isn't optimism, I don't know what to call it. The moral: we "dirty old men" still have a little "boom" left in us after all!

Part II:
Everyday Heroes

The Heroes Among Us

A friend of mine named Hamp Miller, who takes care of my sinuses when we are on the road, gave a talk to our colloquy group about heroes and their response to duty. That inspired me to make this list of some of my heroes. You might want to do the same.

—First, immigrants from anywhere, for doing something to earn equality and advancement.

—Youngsters and oldsters who pursue education vigorously as key to self improvement, with or without tangible reward.

—Persons who actualize Christ's teaching to feed the hungry, clothe the naked, visit those in prison (however prison is defined), etc., "even unto the least of these," and in that category are Habitat, Salvation Army, and other workers who help the least of the least, and the docs and nurses who clean us when we mess ourselves.

—Most elected and appointed officials who give order to our lives, make and enforce rules that secure our safety and well-being, and do the essential work most of us lack the devotion or stamina to do to keep our schools, cities, states, and nation functional.

—School teachers who earn more than they are paid because for them teaching is a calling and a labor that never ends.

—Coaches of youth in whatever sport, girl and boy scout leaders, and other "volunteers" who take up the slack the rest of us create by non-participation.

—The guy or gal who picks up litter, just because it is there and shouldn't be.

—The granddads and grandmoms who shoulder the responsibility of caring for the "accidents" of their progeny.

—Anyone who is uncomfortable when racist or religiously bigoted jokes are told. They don't have to leave the room or chastise, for deliberate embarrassment is never wholly justified; a whisper from an inner voice is sufficient.

—Any man who recognizes the equality—the potential superiority—of women.

The Mayor, Judy Barrett McDonald, in a familiar pose.

And here are some specific examples:

—Abe Lincoln and Harry Truman, because they did what was right according to the Light revealed to them.

—Barry Goldwater, because he was always faithful to his beliefs.

—John F. Kennedy, because he inspired a nation and reminded us that wealth could work for good—and I'll throw in Nelson Rockefeller in a fit of nonpartisanship.

—FDR and LBJ, because those old rascals made us a better people than we wanted to be, or than they were.

—Jonas Salk, and whoever figures out cancer and AIDS, the scourges of our lifetime.

—C.L. Simon, the first black city commissioner in Nacogdoches, whose quiet dignity advanced opportunity for others.

—Mayor Judy, because I know her heart is golden.

—And Hamp Miller, because he got my sinuses home
   from Vienna.
I'm easy—I find heroism everywhere.

Presidents I Have Known

I've known all kinds of presidents, but you might not be interested in Roby Somerford, president of our Rotary Club, or even A.L. Mangham, who once was president of our bank. Both are interesting fellows, and well worth knowing if you need a loan or a friend. But even Roby and A.L. would agree that a POTUS—that's Secret Service code for President of the United States—is above average to know.

I've known six of them. The first was Harry Truman. He wasn't actually still president in 1960 when he came to Baton Rouge and let his Democratic bias overcome his Baptist beginning to urge us all to vote for that Roman Catholic John F. Kennedy. He said it pretty much like that, too. Harry's "give 'em hell" days were behind him, some thought, but I saw fire in his eyes from about the third row of spectators who crowded around the flat-bed truck that served as his stage.

Then came Gerald Ford. We both spoke on a day in the fall of 1974 in the Benson Hotel in downtown Portland, Oregon.

I was there to address a session of the American Folklore Society and he to urge Oregonians to vote in a Republican Congress so they could save the country from Harry's Democrats. It turned out we were scheduled to speak in the same ballroom at the same time. I would have gladly relinquished it, of course, but the hotel knew this so they just changed it without asking me if it was all right. I saw the POTUS when he came through the hotel lobby, and I tell you his hair was redder than it ever looked on TV.

Jimmy Carter came to our campus in the 1980s. He wasn't president anymore, but he had the air of it. My assignment was to get Jimmy to autograph copies of his books for our regents. At the end, I pulled out a poster from the '76 campaign. It featured Jimmy's face with that familiar smile, and read, "Jimmy Carter—*pour le President*—*J'aime Jimmy* [I like Jimmy] *Votez pour le Democrate*." Jimmy grinned when he saw it, and said, "That's from Loosana." You could just tell he was smart. In the question period following his talk, a student asked what one thing he could have done differently to be re-elected in 1980. You could tell Jimmy had considered this before. Quickly he responded, "Send one more helicopter to Desert One." For the callow among us, he was referring to the failed attempt to rescue American embassy hostages in

Iran and a crashed helicopter forced the mission to be scrubbed at a rendezvous site code-named "Desert One."

I met the second Bush first and the first Bush second. George the Younger, who wasn't even governor yet, much less a POTUS, came to town to campaign for Kay Bailey Hutchison for the Senate. George the Elder spoke on our campus *after* he was president. Both were pretty nice fellows while they were in town.

Finally, in 1995, I accompanied my mayor-wife to a meeting of the National League of Cities in the nation's capital. She sneaked me into the plenary session addressed by William Jefferson Blythe Clinton. This was long before the world worried over the blue dresses of interns and such. He made a pretty good speech, though. He told us he wasn't as bad as Newt Gingrich, who had spoken to us earlier, had said he was.

You can see now that I only actually met one POTUS—for about five minutes—and was an "extra" in crowded scenes with five others. I suppose even that is a higher average than some of my fellow citizens. I have lunch with Roby and A.L. about once a week, and am much more likely to get a loan from *either* of them than all six of these other presidents combined.

Teachers I Have Known

We are all products of our teachers, and we have many of them. From parents we learn, for good or ill, language, habits, attitudes. Older siblings and school buddies also provide other lessons of life, and sometimes Sunday School teachers or preachers try a hand at bringing us along the higher path. But just now I am celebrating schoolteachers—the ladies and gentlemen who took up the work as a profession and more than earned their salaries. I am going to call some names here.

Mrs. Henrich was my seventh grade Texas history teacher. You can tell from that name that she was Prussian, and her exacting and demanding methods came right out of *Whermacht* heritage. But she noted a spark of interest in this son of a Scotsman and led me and pushed me into a love of history not yet extinguished.

I changed ethnicity for my eighth grade American history teacher, Mrs. Dugas, whose Frenchness brought a more delicate touch to the process. Bob Warren, my high school history teacher, for whom I later had the pleasure of writing a letter of recommendation for graduate school *after* I had completed my own degrees, taught high school classes using the college lecture method and more than prepared me for them when I actually enrolled in one, then two more universities for advanced degrees.

Some good teachers, mentors, and friends in college followed, too many to mention. The table turns, and now I look back on forty-three years of fronting classrooms at LSU, Murray State in Kentucky, Central Washington in that state, and mostly at Stephen F. Austin State University. And I wonder if I hindered more than helped.

Some students who passed through my classes, including graduate students, have made considerable successes. One became president of the American Medical Association. Two are presidents of banks. One edits a national magazine. Several are college and university teachers, and three have returned as regents of Stephen F. Austin State University. Several have written books. Quite a few students have told me that their fathers or mothers were in my classes twenty-five or thirty-five years or so ago—and I swear I'll quit when one says "grandmother was in your class in 1964." It could happen any year now. Do the math.

What I make of this, after over four decades and about 10,000 students, is that at least I didn't get in the way.

God Bless John Wayne

Early in the 1970s, I introduced a class titled "John Wayne and the American West" in what we called a mini-mester, a three-week hiatus between Spring and Summer I sessions. The three-hour classes allowed an hour's lecture on some western theme followed by a John Wayne film illustrating that theme.

This quickly became a popular course; "popular," in academe, is measured by enrollment. Usually seventy-five or so students enrolled, though some learned to their sorrow that the course involved exams and grades and such.

After the demise of the mini-mester at our college, we dropped the course for several reasons, one of which was the death of the main character on June 11, 1979. I thought interest in Wayne would wane then, but I was mistaken. More than two decades later, Wayne remains an icon of America, still so recognizable that his image is used in modern beer commercials without identification. The agencies apparently assumed that even customers unborn at any point in his lifetime would be familiar with his four-square persona.

They are correct. Twenty-five years after his death Wayne still ranks second on the all-time list of box-office champions. I think I know why.

One evening we watched a rerun of "The Comancheros," an old movie starring Wayne which provides an excellent example of his delivery of expository speech. Pausing where there were not commas or periods in the script and running other words together where such punctuation brakes did occur, Wayne developed a deliberate and distinctive "gait" to his speech. And he could instill the simplest statement with more sincerity than a carload of method actors.

Consider this wonderful line. Wayne plays a Texas Ranger who has co-star Stuart Whitman in custody. After they share adventures and save each other's lives, Whitman's character asks the Ranger to let him escape. "Can't," says Wayne, "took an oath." Says Whitman, "Them's just words."

Comes now the Golden Message from Olympus, spoken so softly the audience strains to hear and delivered with direct eye contact so we voyeurs can't miss their solemnity: "Words are what men live by . . . words they say and mean."

James Edward Grant, Wayne's favorite screenwriter, scripted that sentence but what gave it meaning was the persona Wayne had developed over the decades through scores of films.

By the time "The Comancheros" was released, audiences knew what to expect from a film in which Wayne appeared: there would be lots of action but, in the end, good prevailed over evil, and Wayne's character would personify American patriotism. That was the principal reason why Wayne became, and remains, a major force in American and world popular culture and still my all time favorite movie personality.

"Words are what men live by . . . words they say and mean" may have been written by someone else, but Wayne gave those words power. Hearing them again almost washes away my cynicism about the downslide in American integrity and just plain good taste, especially in entertainment. Almost.

Best I can learn, Wayne did live by the words he said and meant.

What If I Had Practiced as Much as Van Cliburn?

I don't think I knew what a "nerd" was, back in the 1940s, when Mother wanted me to take piano lessons, but I'm pretty sure about the fear of being perceived as one by the other clients of French Junior High School. That anxiety, and a void in talent, kept me from winning that Tchaikovsky contest in Russia even before Van Cliburn did so.

I'll bet Van practiced every day, whether his mother wanted him to or not. He probably enjoyed it, after receiving some kind of assurance in Kilgore that it would make him world famous and rich. I, on the other hand, had no such prescience.

Mother enrolled me in Miss Shoemaker's piano class against my wishes, and for all I know over the objections of Miss Shoemaker as well. If she had none in September, surely some had developed by December. We two condemned souls met twice weekly for thirty-minute lessons which tested our endurance and tolerance.

"Bend your fingers," Miss Shoemaker would order. "Don't look at your hands—look at the music." "Sit up straight." "Don't you ever practice?"

"Yes, ma'am," I would lie, for my Mother raised no fool. A liar, maybe, but not a fool.

And so it concluded after an embarrassing year-end recital when the serious students played well and I . . . played less well.

I have just described a tragedy in my life, for now I would give a pretty penny to be able to play the piano half as well as Van. Truth told, I'd like to be able to chord like Fats Domino. I can play a one-finger melody line, with a double-octave bass, all the way through "Too Young" and about half of "Old Man River" if I leave out some of the bass. I can pick out the chorus of "Dixie" and do pretty well until I get to the final "look away, Dixie land"—then I have to go pretty slow not to sound a clunker. This is not what Mother had in mind.

In high school, I remember a Roger something—I can't recall his full name—who could play any song you could think of. Roger never read a single note of music in his life, but his "ear," as he identified the source of his power, directed his fingers to merge with the keyboard and produce as much music as you could stand. I also remember lots of girls standing around the piano when old Roger played. I wish I could play as well as Roger, even with my "ear."

I disappointed Mother, but she loved me anyway. As bad, at least, I disappointed me. I'm sure I never would have been as good as Van. But if I had practiced more, and somehow passed through that threshold that separates the dreamers from the doers, I could at least play "Dixie" and "The Battle Hymn" and "Amazing Grace" and maybe even a little Tchaikovsky.

Mother would be proud. And the girls around the piano would like it, too.

World War II
Home Front

The first of the "Where were you when . . ." questions I can answer concerns the Japanese attack on Pearl Harbor on December 7, 1941.

I had just begun the educational process at Averell Elementary School in Beaumont. That big Philco radio that focused the living room prior to the advent of television told us that war had found us. I remember my grandmother crying softly and the strained countenances of my mother and aunt, though I really did not understand why.

The next four years provided more memories of World War II, such as:

—Ration books, issued by the Office of Price
   Administration to every member of the household,
   necessary to purchase such commodities as shoes and
   sugar. No ration stamp, no purchase, at least legally,
   but of course some unscrupulous individuals partici-

pated in a "black market." The purchase of meat required "red points," or dime-sized red plastic disks that equated to so many points per pound allowed.

— "A" or "T" stickers in auto or truck windshields, indicating the amount of gasoline allowable for that vehicle. And gasoline cost about twenty cents per gallon.

—War Bonds, Series "E," the $18.75 deducted from Daddy's paycheck that purchased a document worth $25 in ten years. And the little books we school kids filled with a savings stamp every week, at ten cents a stamp, until we, too, had helped pay for the war and put a little nest-egg aside. We didn't care that this was the government's way to finance the war and slow inflation, but we did anticipate the agonizingly slow compounding of the interest.

—V-Mail, or victory mail, letters received from servicemen overseas that had been photographically diminished to lessen the load of hauling so many letters from America's millions of men in far-flung duty stations. And marvel of marvels, they traveled all that way without a postage stamp.

—Scrap drives of everything from rubber to all metals, newspapers, even animal fat saved from cooking. I remember pulling my wagon door to door collecting newspapers to be turned in for reprocessing, but I don't remember ever hearing the word "recycling." I also remember searching for discarded cigarette packages so we could separate what we called "tin foil" used to seal the pack for freshness. We rolled it into balls and turned it in. I also remember lines outside stores on the one or two days per week that cigarettes were available for purchase.

—Blackouts. When the siren sounded, lights were cut off. If any had to be illuminated, blankets covered all windows lest the air-raid warden, usually a neighbor empowered to patrol the area, knocked to issue the warning that we were aiding the feared German bombers that never appeared.

What I don't remember is much complaining about these inconveniences. America had a different vision, then.

The First Time I Ate in an Integrated Restaurant

Some things are so extraordinary, so shocking, they fix themselves in the mind forever. Time stops. A little camera in your brain freezes that moment and you can take it out anytime and examine it.

For instance, I remember exactly where, and when, I sat down to a meal in a public restaurant at the same time an African American family was having lunch. This extraordinary event happened in Jasper, Texas, in 1965. I expect it had taken a year for the public accommodations portion of the Civil Rights Act of 1964 to work itself to East Texas.

Younger folks may think this quaint. It happens every day now, in every community in America. But in 1965, it was an event. I joined a segregated world in Beaumont, Texas, and attended segregated schools, at least until Lamar College integrated its undergraduate program in the fall of my sophomore year in 1956. Separate schools and separate public drinking fountains and restrooms were the norm. I didn't think about that much then; it was just the way things were. I don't know exactly when it occurred to me that some adjustments were overdue.

I would like to think it began when I crossed a protest line of "Segregation Forever" advocates at Lamar to attend class. I might not be able to claim that I marched with Martin, as so many later did, but could I say that I crossed that line because I believed so strongly in equal rights? Not really. I crossed it because I knew that a college degree would help me escape a dead-end job as an oilfield roustabout.

Somewhere, sometime, I did change. I think everyone in my generation, black *and* white, still has to battle latent racism. It permeated our raising, so it is a stubborn critter. Our little daily victories are worth celebrating.

Sometime I am going to tell you about those victories, about my friend C.L. Simon, who had to go to college in Colorado because schools in Texas would not register him. Or about the Revs. Isaiah Nordsworthy and John Hardin—in that very same Jasper, where I ate my first integrated meal and James Byrd's life ended behind a pickup truck—whose love of God extends to all His creatures, including whites like me.

About that meal, in Jasper, with a black family eating at the next table: I don't remember the food. It was probably something that tasted good that doctors tell me not to eat anymore. Do you know what happened? Nothing. Our families finished our meals, paid our bills, and went on our way.

Now isn't that amazing? Isn't that a victory worth remembering?

My Maw Was Born in Arkansas

This is a tribute to all mothers, but especially to my own, Pernemia Tulia Cowan McDonald Tucker. As Bear Bryant advised: "Call yore Mama. I sure wish I could call mine."

Mother was born in Pine Bluff, Arkansas, in May of a year I am not going to share with you, but since I was born in 1935 you can subtract a few years and get pretty close. She greeted the world in Arkansas for no better reason than that her father, John Cowan, a brakeman on the Cotton Belt line, worked out of the railroad's headquarters there. Following his death in 1919 in a train crash, Mama Cowan, my Aunt Jonnie, and Mother moved south to Vernon Parish, Louisiana, to join the household of Frederick Craft and his wife, my maternal great-grandparents.

Mother completed high school in Beaumont, Texas, after a good deal of the family had moved there during the 1920s seeking work and release from an agricultural depression

My mother, Nem Tucker, with her "college professor" son come to talk to her Study Club.

that had gripped the South since the Civil War, then worsened after World War I. The Babe, Mildred Didrikson, the century's greatest woman athlete, was a classmate at Beaumont High School when both were graduated in 1929. (If you are still figuring age, there were only eleven grades in school then).

Mother married Archie McDonald, which explains me, and after his death in 1944, she went to work to support us as a telephone operator. She spent lunch breaks across the street in the Enterprise Café, where she met my next father, George Harvie Tucker, which accounts for my brothers

George and John and my sister Nancy. Please note the absence of the word "step" in any of these relationships—though technically true, no such distinction was made then and I allow none now.

After her remarriage, Mother made a home for Daddy Tucker and the rest of us until we were all grown and gone. She worked a while in the parish library and became an avid clubwoman, especially in Eastern Star and her beloved Study Club. Her annual invitations for me to speak to one or the other were never declined. Adopting my brothers' better example, we called her every Sunday afternoon for the last two decades of her life—except for the year she lived with us so the good doctors of Nacogdoches could help her conquer lymphoma. She did that, then left us the next year after losing a bout with an impacted colon.

A thousand times I have wanted to ask Mother something, usually as mundane as the identity of a relative in an old picture; sometimes things more meaningful, more important. It would be wonderful now, to call her, to hear her voice brighten when the prodigal identified himself, and to say, "I love you" one more time. I never did that enough.

From me and the Bear, even though this may not be that special day in May: "Call yore Mama!"

/

My Two Fathers

Lately I have been reflecting on the business of paternity, especially the gentlemen who fathered me.

I have few memories of my paternal grandfather, Madison McDonald, who passed away when I was seven years old, and none at all of my maternal grandfather, John Cowan, a brakeman on the Cotton Belt line who perished in a train crash long before I was born.

My father was Archie McDonald, born in Sugartown, Louisiana. I remember him sitting on a stool in the living room of the house we occupied with two aunts and mother's mother, strumming a guitar. I have a small scar where he lanced an infection with his pocketknife. I have his hat, his pocket watch, some of his barber tools, and his name, and I remember his face and frame mostly from photos which have reinforced my mental image of him for so long it is difficult to separate those captured moments from the vital man who once lived.

My father, Archie McDonald "the dandy," crossing Pearl Street in downtown Beaumont.

That image is of a dandy, neatly dressed in suit and tie, always wearing a hat in candid shots but showing dark, wavy hair in indoor, posed portraits. He followed various trades; I remember best his barbering and livestock trading but also remember us peddling chickens and pecans when he grew too weak for physical labor. He let me think I earned my first bicycle catching chickens in a cage in our truck which we sold live at neighborhood groceries.

I remember a sharp blow of discipline here and there, doubtless deserved and owed partially to his declining health and battle with mortality. And I remember a poem he wrote and Mother preserved about how proud he was to have me as his son. Daddy died on June 4, 1944, five months shy of my ninth birthday.

In time, Mother married again. Her choice was George Tucker, an electrician at Pennsylvania Shipyard in Beaumont. They met in the Enterprise Cafe, near where she worked as a telephone operator. It was his first, and only, marriage. Tucker, as everyone called him, was certainly an improvement over the other suitor she brought home for approval. He was called Tarzan. 'Nough said.

George Tucker became Daddy. After the war Daddy worked for Kelly's Dairy as a salesman on the commercial route, and I often accompanied him on Saturday. This brought us into contact with some of his previous paramours—waitresses or cafe operators. He always introduced me simply as "my son" and never explained, at least in my presence, the "step" nature of our relationship. It never entered the picture, not then, not later, and does not now. But it did shock the old girl friends, who must have wondered where I had been hidden when they courted.

George Tucker could work and whistle at the same time. He once told me that he never knew what it was to tire until past thirty years of age. He grew up in cotton middles in Navarro County and came to Beaumont during the Depression, as had our family, to seek work. Work was his solution for all problems, yet family meant more to him.

My second father, Geroge Harvie Tucker, heading shrimp in the backyard in Lake Charles, La.

Funerals, weddings, family gathering, he did the heavy lifting, so to speak, of getting ready and cleaning up.

Daddy taught me to shave. He held my hand through the trials of teenage. My sons were his first grandchildren, and he loved them without reservation. He raised another man's son and never counted the cost.

For a long time it gave me pain when I heard Eddie Arnold sing his country-music tearjerker, "My Son Calls Another Man Daddy." But maturity made me grateful that I had two fathers and wish that I had been as good at parenting as either of them. And I hope there is a good daddy out there for every boy or girl who needs one.

Daddy Tucker left us in the winter of 1987. That great heart had weakened and a stroke did the rest. I can hear him still, whistling, or calling out, in old age, "Come sit with me and talk awhile." Lord, I wish I could hear that again.

Aunt Jonnie

I doubt if they are unique to Southern families; on the other hand, that is the case with all of them I have known, and so my judgment may be regional. I know it is personal. I am talking about maiden aunts, especially of an earlier time.

Nowadays, many women prefer to remain "maiden," or at least unmarried. To their grandparents' generation, however, the Great Expectation for females was that they would grow up and marry. Careers were limited to "school teaching," nursing, or clerking, with even these posts considered temporary until marriage or as a supplemental salary afterwards.

What then, to do, with the unmarried females without careers? My Aunt Jonnie was such a lady. Unlike Aunt Vennie, the family matriarch who supported us all financially and just as often emotionally, Aunt Jonnie remained at home. I do not believe that she was ever gainfully employed except by family.

Aunt Jonnie had a weight problem which doubtless contributed to her circumstance. She became the primary

Aunt Jonnie Lois Cowan with me in 1945. I'm wearing my cousin's sailor hat.

housekeeper for our limb of the family tree and caregiver for the whole family. If Aunt Thelma fell and cut her knee, Aunt Jonnie was summoned, regardless of her own plans, to "stay" with that family and do the cooking, washing, and cleaning, and child care because "she had nothing else to do." No job, you see, or other real reason, to keep her from going. Best of all, she always went with a willing heart. And no pay.

Aunt Jonnie never learned to drive an automobile, so she was dependent on others for all transportation and relished her once-a-week grocery buying trip with Roberta Cole, who lived across the street and provided the wheels for their excursions. Without income, Aunt Jonnie used Aunt Vennie's money to buy our food.

My Aunt Jonnie marked me, for she was the one always at home when I came in from school. We sparred some—she always wanted to serve dinner fairly early, "to get it over with," she would say, and the rebellious teenager would respond, "But I don't eat to 'get it over with.'"

When I had measles, Aunt Jonnie told me it was leprosy, that dread disease I had heard about from the Bible but of course had never seen, and it scared the heck out of me. Because I wanted green beans at every meal, she told me I would turn green, and I half believed her. But when I hurt, she was there. We would argue over dominoes and card games to the point of tears and pouting, but I was never wrong in her eyes if the dispute involved a playmate.

In that South, families kept their maiden aunts close, in the home and in the heart. Aunt Jonnie was one of those who formed me, back in the 1930s and 1940s. She nursed us to the end, and the memory of her nurtures us still.

Aunt Vennie

She was born Nancy Lovenia Craft in Vernon Parish, Louisiana, in 1884, but we called her Aunt Vennie. A more generous soul never graced the earth. A measure of that generosity was that in Aunt Vennie's eyes, I did no wrong. Every person should have that blessing. Of course, this put the green into the eyes of every last cousin I had in the world, but so what?

Aunt Vennie's siblings, born to a German family who farmed near Leesville, Louisiana, numbered about ten. She was the first in her family to attend college, and did so in Natchitoches. Aunt Vennie moved to Beaumont, Texas, early in the 1920s and worked at the Star Store, a laboring man's department store. Eventually her household included her sister, my parents, my mother's sister—Aunt Jonnie—and this perfect child.

Aunt Vennie was the family matriarch. She paid the rent until the landlord sold her the house after she became office manager at the Star Store. My father, whose life resembled that

of Jimmy Rodgers (including the TB), helped out as long as he could, but essentially the source of our support was Aunt Vennie. She never married, so I received all the "mothering" this remarkable woman had to give. It was more like "grandmothering," for my Mother had to provide the discipline and Aunt Vennie supplied the ice cream afterwards.

Aunt Vennie—Nancy Lovenia Craft —the matriarch of the family who supported us all financially and emotionally.

It was Aunt Vennie who supported my candy habit, bought my Cub Scout uniforms and baseball gloves, paid for my clothes. It was she who showed the most concern when I was ill, the most determination that I should be educated. Since I rode a city bus to school, we developed a habit, at her invitation, that I collect her at her office when school let out each day. We walked around the corner for "coffee and pie" at the Piccadilly Cafeteria.

Sad to say, I was not worthy of her unqualified conviction that I was, if not actually perfect, a pretty swell kid. Spoiled is what I was, and, in the way of the world, when I learned the word, flawed. Aunt Vennie thought otherwise, and I confess that I worked a little harder at self-discipline because I could not bear to have her find those flaws. I reckon she knew, but in a way her expectation resulted in a greater effort on my part.

I could not have gone to college without Aunt Vennie's emotional and financial support. I would not have been able to attend graduate school without similar help from Aunt Vennie and my wife of forty-eight winters and counting. When we two produced children, they became my successors but not my replacements in Aunt Vennie's affection. She helped me appreciate the unlimited reservoir of love right on through the day she left us in 1970.

All this is inadequate for what I really wanted to say in this tribute to my Aunt Vennie. I am too close, too involved, still, to say "I love you" as well as I wish.

I hope you had an Aunt Vennie, too. Everyone deserves at least one person who sees more in them than they see in themselves.

The Big Bopper

Early in the 1950s, when I still worried about acne and wondered how and where I would get the courage to ask Julianne what's-her-name for a date, Beaumont's radio station KTRM aired a balm for the baffled beginning at 9:00 P.M. each evening. The program's format of "easy listening" music for those in love—and those who wanted to be—continued until midnight, but Mother never let me stay up that late.

This program starkly contrasted with the remainder of the station's fare, which was "hillbilly" followed by "country" followed by more "hillbilly" followed by more. . . . This was punctuated with Tommy O'Brien on sports and another now-forgotten fellow reporting news off the wires every few hours.

Then, at 9:00 P.M., frenzy ceased. The mellow voice of disk jockey J.P. Richardson wafted through the mysteries of broadcast radio to the little brown, plastic, all-AM receiver in my room. A slow instrumental piece provided background while our old friend greeted us and gently eased into the evening's program of soothing, almost pacifying, "easy listening" music.

Were we fooled! We knew that Buddy Holly and Bill Haley and some kid named Presley were upsetting the musical world, but we knew not that in another, secret life, J.P. Richardson metamorphosed into The Big Bopper, a rock-'n'roller more interested in Chantilly Lace and pony tails hanging down than in listening easy about anything.

For a while the masquerade continued. Richardson kept his "day job"—or more rightly his "night job"—with KTRM while he developed this schizoid character. We worried over his well-being when he set a then-record of broadcasting for over ninety-six consecutive hours from the lobby of the Jefferson Theatre. He even had the prop of an ambulance waiting to whisk him to the hospital in case of collapse, and he did get to ride in it when the ordeal was over.

The "Mr. Hyde" side won out when The Big Bopper and "Chantilly Lace" hit the big time. Only then, did we—or at least I—learn of his dual personality. I followed Richardson's short if spectacular career in rock'n'roll avidly until he boarded that ill-fated airplane with Holly and Richie Valance on a snowy night to make the next gig.

As a songwriter put it, the music died that night when Buddy Holly's plane went down. For Beaumonters, the silencing of J.P. Richardson's, or The Big Bopper's, music was a personal tragedy. The listening wasn't so easy anymore.

I hear "Chantilly Lace" less frequently now, most often as background in a movie such as "Pretty Woman." I wonder, if Buddy and Richie and The Big Bopper had survived that flight, what might we think now of J.P. Richardson? A boy grows up and becomes a man, but he still listens easy, and he still wonders.

When 'Republican' Wasn't Cool

There really was a time, children, when no Republicans—or hardly any—lived in Texas. This might take some faith on your part, but go along with a historian on this for awhile.

I'll admit some of the Democrats in those days *sounded* like Republicans when they cussed Mr. Roosevelt, but they always voted in the Democratic primary, and anyway there weren't any Republicans for whom they could have voted, except in presidential election years, because all the candidates were Democrats, too.

Those were the "good old days" for the donkey party. Nearly everyone claimed to be a "yellow dog Democrat" who would vote even for such a critter as that in preference to a representative of the party that whipped the Rebels in 1865 and caused the Great Depression. Texas Democrats even gave Republican names, such as Hoover Hogs, to jackrabbits and armadillos, table fare during the 1930s and evidence of the lack of prosperity promised but unprovided by Hoover's party.

Somehow the Grand Old Party kept on going. Even without Texans' votes they managed to elect every president after the Civil War except one, a damnyankee Democrat from New York named Grover Cleveland, until 1912; dominated the presidency again in the 1920s; took a licking from Mr. Roosevelt and Mr. Truman in the 1930s and 1940s; and then won most of the time for the rest of the twentieth century.

Republicans found a crack in the Solid South in the presidential election in 1928 when three states, including Texas, defected to Hoover. Texans reunited as Democrats until 1952, when Ike widened the breach, then they started voting for all kinds of Nixons, Reagans, and Bushes. Republicans didn't do so well in Texas, Congress-wise, for a long time, and no governors and few legislators, judges, or sheriffs would admit to Republicanism.

Then, things happened. Things involving civil rights, guns, government regulations, taxes, police actions abroad, judicial activism . . . the list is long.

Before the Democrats knew what had happened, most of our governors, Congress members and legislators, even judges and sheriffs, suffered an epiphany, a real Damascus

Road experience. They realized that they really had been Republicans all along. Some just announced that the scales had dropped from their eyes and went right on judging and sheriffing. Others bravely admitted they had seen the light, though usually they swore it was the Democrats who had changed, not them.

So now we have the New New Texas. In the first New Texas, right after the War for Southern Independence, everyone thought he had to be a Democrat to have local control. But in the New New Texas, we understand that we should have been Republicans all along.

There really is a time, children, when no Democrats—or hardly any—live in Texas.

Harry's Bar

I am going to take you to visit Harry's bar in Paris. Not *the* Harry's Bar famous in Paris and every major European capital. This one is on the Rue d'la'Opera. It is where Harry lives.

Harry is a German Shepherd. We made his acquaintance seven or eight years ago on our annual Fact-Finding Mission to the Continent with friends and colleagues. Sore of foot from too much walking to see the sights of Paris, we appropriated several of the little sidewalk tables that tourists love to occupy and try to look like genuine Parisians.

We ordered glasses of the local nectar so we could stay planted long enough to rest, and along came Harry. It must be a rule that Parisians are required to own a dog, for they are everywhere, even in restaurants. France is also famed for food. Harry and food figure prominently in this story.

Several other patrons tossed Harry scraps—French fries, bread crust, whatever—which he snapped up with zest.

Harry, the dog in Paris that fascinates me so.

Seeking to make friends, always a good idea with large dogs—I offered him a cookie. Now this particular cookie was one I had brought from home on orders from my doctor. It was fat free.

Harry sniffed it, took it in his mouth—and expectorated the thing right back to me. I swear Harry said it tasted like cardboard. Needless to say, we became friends.

Two years later, Tommie Lowery, Judy, and I walked by that brassier again and went inside to see if Harry was there. Sure enough, Harry was walking among the tables, mooching. We ordered French fries and Harry ate most of them. A waiter said, "Watch this." He popped a top off a bottle of Perrier and waved the cap. Harry was alert. The waiter tossed the cap, and Harry caught it—between his front paws. You thought I would say that he caught it in his mouth, didn't you?

Two years ago, same gig, but this time with Cousin Millie. Millie couldn't believe that we now had a Tradition of finding Harry on each trip to Paris. She tried to prepare us for the possibility of dognapping, demise, or disappearance. We went in, but no Harry could we see. We asked. "*Oui,* he is asleep under the counter." They roused Harry, who came out to claim his French fries.

Last spring we returned a fourth time, and again found Harry asleep. He rose, more slowly than before, a little shaky on his feet. He brought his green squeeze toy to Judy, then lay down near us and went back to sleep.

Now I have some conclusions and a question.

First, if a dog is smart, he will live in Paris, for a dog's life is good in Paris. So is a person's life, for that matter.

Second, I swear that Harry remembers us, as we remember him. The Louvre and *Tour Effle* are fine, but in Paris, I always want to see Harry.

Finally, why can't I have French fries and still grow old like Harry?

Older Women

Our friend Angela Key sent me some thoughts from another—and much more famous—curmudgeon, Andy Rooney, singing the praises of "older women." Now I realize I am on shaky ground, so I'm going to re-identify the category as "mature women." I'm not sure where Angela fits on the scale, but I expect she qualifies.

Anyway, I agree 100 percent with Andy's advocacy, but empirical evidence, gathered after exhaustive observation, causes me to question one of his conclusions. Andy says that "most older women cook well." That may be true, but the problem is getting them to do it. Most of the mature women of *my* acquaintance gave up this activity long ago.

Still, I think Andy's basic conclusion is correct, and so I offer these arguments in support without borrowing further from *his* evidence. After all, Andy is a New Yorker who works in Manhattan, and I am a son of the South. Obviously, our empiricism focuses on completely different branches of the species:

—Mature Southern women generally groom themselves appropriately to the occasion. They will wear the most paint-stained, pull-over shirt mismatched with baggy shorts to pull a water hose around the backyard but wouldn't think of leaving the house, even on an inconsequential mission, without fresh lipstick, attention to their hair, and neat clothing. Ratchet up the significance of the occasion, and we are talking hose, heels, and hallelujah at how good they look to an old man.

—Mature Southern women display diverse personalities. In any *public* situation, they are well behaved, demure, even pious in church, and judgmental—especially of the nastiness of the males in their lives. But in *private*, when the world has gone away, a seamier, steamier self that revels in a little earthiness appears—if you are lucky.

—Mature Southern women have an inner voice—something beyond instinct—that tells them not just when but how to react to the endangerment of mate or offspring which enables them to be simultaneously ferocious in defense and condemnatory for getting yourself into that mess in the first place.

By now you may have drawn two conclusions: First, that I don't have the slightest understanding of women—mature,

Southern, or otherwise. Second, that I have been talking primarily about one particular woman.

I have studied this woman for a long time, and while I am no closer to the understanding of which we spoke than when I began this study in 1957, I have reached this conclusion: It makes one believe in God to realize that you have found that one person in the world who is willing to put up with you.

Funerals

All of us have too much unwanted experience with funerals, and one of the saddening aspects of maturing is that we find ourselves attending them frequently. We lament the loss of loved one, friend, co-worker, or person of whatever consequence in our lives, but the worst part, I think, is the confrontation with our own mortality.

I am not comfortable with this topic, yet I feel compelled to address it. I'll leave it to the psychologists among you to figure out why.

I have attended funerals of every conceivable family and friendship connection, and I have conducted three services myself. I do not recommend it. All were attended from a sense of duty—I never *wanted* to be in that church or funeral home or cemetery. That same circumstance has led me to accept assignment as eulogist or obituary writer for two dear friends, and I certainly do not want *that* work to come soon.

I had one friend who felt so strongly about this that he *never* attended funerals. He returned the favor and arranged a family-only service for himself. Another friend wants us there but has requested that his "ole buddies" bend an elbow in remembrance of him as soon as possible after the service.

I have observed some things about the final rites that warrant these comments:

First, there isn't much difference between believers and non-believers in grieving by survivors. Loss of loved ones is loss, whether or not one believes they are with the Lord. I am certain some survivors are comforted by that assurance, but all hurt.

Second, many services bring us to such grief that we break or bend, and it is the bending I think of now—that time when we gather back at the house around tables laden with casseroles contributed by friends who don't know what else to do for us. We recall good times, and laughter, almost giddiness, comes. We bend lest we break.

Third, the conductor of the service—preacher, priest, rabbi, or eulogist—should know, and I mean pretty well, the subject of the occasion.

A couple of years ago our family attended the funeral for my wife's uncle, a pillar of his Baptist church. He grew up in that church, was baptized and married there, saw children and grandchildren baptized in its sanctuary. But the new pastor knew him not—kept calling him *Mr*. Spencer, instead of Jimmy. Not knowing what else to do, he used the time to try to save the souls of those yet living.

This incensed my wife. I have to tell you that she is a remarkably accomplished woman. She served as mayor of our town near a decade and is involved in everything. Our area has a preacher—let's call him Pastor Jones. Pastor Jones so disapproved of women in positions of authority that he and some of his believers picketed in protest of her. So in Judy's instructions to me and our son, she raged, "When my time comes, if Kyle Childress (our pastor) can't do it, you get Father Young, you get Allen Reid (another pastor in our town she likes), you get *somebody* who *knows* me!"

Christopher brought us to that state of giddiness we needed. "Mother," said he, "if you die on us, we are going to get Pastor Jones." That ought to keep her going for a hundred years.

Greetings We Just Know Are Not Going to Lead to Good News

We communicate in many ways, including the obvious one of talking to each other, but also through body language, inflection, and, sometimes, by remaining silent. Then there are some communications you just know are not going to end in good news. Consider these:

Phone rings. "Mr. McDonald, this is the Nacogdoches Police Department . . ."

Phone rings again, "Mr. McDonald, this is the Home Protective Service in Houston and your burglar alarm has been activated . . ."

A letter from the Internal Revenue Service begins, "Mr. McDonald, a review of your records indicates a failure to report income in 2001 and you owe $17,523.24, plus interest and penalties . . ." with never an "oops, we're sorry" that they miscalculated a rollover as a payout . . .

Doctor Ledet shuts off the treadmill during your stress test and says, "Looks like we have a little more work to do . . ."

Back in the 1950s comes a letter from Selective Service that starts out "Greetings!". . .

A note scrawled on your exam book or term paper in blood-red ink screams, "Nice try, but . . ."

Your wife (or husband) begins a conversation with "We need to talk . . . about the kids . . . about the bills . . . about your (fill in as many disgusting habits as may be appropriate)," or perhaps the even more ominous "We need to talk . . ." that drifts off with a sigh about the futility of it all . . .

Or she is flying in a small plane coming home from Austin, and the pilot blurts out, "I hate to tell you this, but either we are out of gas or the gauge isn't working . . ."

The auto/television/appliance repair person calls and reports, "This is going to run a little more than we thought . . ."

The insurance company representative says, "I *thought* your policy covered that, but . . ."

Any phone call between midnight and dawn, regardless of *how* it begins.

Most of the above was autobiographical. But here is a conversation starter that is not likely to happen to me ever again: "Honey, we're pregnant . . ."

Afterword:
The Way We Were

When Judy and I saw the film "The Way We Were" and heard Ms. Streisand sing "Memories," I identified instantly and completely with the movie and the song. I know I do not resemble Robert Redford, of course, but we do share memories, recollections of a simpler time and place.

Most of the memories included in this collection focus on the 1940s and 1950s and on my family and the way we lived back then. I don't know if we were a "typical" family for the times. Some we knew enjoyed more resources, some survived with less, but in so many ways we lived a shared experience. We all survived our country's deepest economic depression and its greatest war, and we embraced the renewed "normalcy" of Dwight Eisenhower's near decade in the presidency.

Although I adapt to each new decade, utilize its technology, and find amusement in recurring fads, that earlier time marked me. My ambitions, hopes, and values crystallized back then. Not all those ambitions eventuated and doubtless I have compromised some of the values on the way to now. But hope remains, and looking back to my beginnings makes it seem possible still.

I hope you have enjoyed returning to that time and place with me.